The Parent's Guide to Self-Harm

*What Parents
Need to Know*

To my three wonderful daughters

The Parent's Guide to Self-Harm

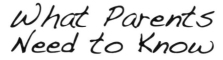

What Parents
Need to Know

Jane Smith

L I O N

Published by Lion Books
an imprint of
Lion Hudson plc
Wilkinson House, Jordan Hill Road,
Oxford OX2 8DR, England
www.lionhudson.com/lion
ISBN 978 0 7459 5570 4
e-ISBN 978 0 7459 5895 8

First edition 2012

A catalogue record for this book is available from the British Library

Printed and bound in Great Britain, June 2012, LH26

Contents

Acknowledgments

I'd like to thank all the parent contributors who have made this book one of such personal insight by being so willing to share their stories and recall their emotions. I'd like to pay tribute to the openness and courage of my daughter Imogen Smith who, having found recovery, encouraged me to write this book. I'm very grateful to the staff, trustees, and medical advisors at ABC, notably Dr Dee Dawson, Jackie Disbury, and Nicola Rance. I couldn't have done without the support and advice of Dr Jane Sutton, and the good practice of Dr Matthew Dolman and Dr Ros King. Many thanks also go to Ali Hull, David Moloney, Julie Frederick, Jessica Tinker, and Leisa Nugent at Lion Hudson for their wisdom and expertise.

About ABC's Parent Helpline

Anorexia and Bulimia Care (ABC) is a UK organization that has been helping people with eating disorders and related self-harm for more than twenty years. I joined ABC in 2004 in order to run their parent helpline, and since then it has received calls from thousands of parents, all loving and supporting their children of varying ages through an eating disorder and self-harm. The rise in the number of parents wanting to talk about self-harm has meant that ABC has created a new, separate confidential helpline dedicated to self-harm, and a befriending service run by parents who have supported a loved one through to recovery. Parents phone at various stages: during the initial days of discovery and worry; while trying to manage and accept self-harm, through the wait for treatment; or through treatment itself and towards recovery. When they call, parents are looking for advice, comfort, and encouragement from people who have been where they are now, and who really understand what they're going through.

Parents want to speak to people who are prepared to listen and answer their questions. Often they are deeply distressed, worried, and worn out. Most feel alone, hopeless, and unsupported. They want to know what they can do to help their child overcome self-harm, or what NHS treatment is available. They want to know about the different types of counselling available: individual, group, or family therapy.

Whatever their different needs, they all desperately want to share their story, talk about how they are responding to their child's and family's needs, and discuss methods they could try to prevent any further harm happening to their son or daughter. Being informed and having suggestions gives hope, and our helpline offers ongoing help and hope to anyone who needs it. We hear from mums and dads; from step-parents, siblings, aunts and uncles, grandparents, friends, girlfriends, boyfriends, and teachers.

Some are single parents trying to cope alone. Others have their own health problems – sometimes serious – or are already supporting someone in the family with a major illness or disability. Sometimes the child who self-harms has additional needs and may suffer with another long-term illness or condition.

We hear from parents of children from the age of seven onwards, through the teenage years to young adults. Many are trying to support an adult child who lives independently, and this brings specific problems, as they are often excluded from their child's difficulties and any treatment. Despite their different circumstances, all the parents want to understand and help their children through the terrible ordeal towards full recovery, as well as to find a little relief from the overwhelming fear, sadness, and isolation that they experience.

Introduction

This is a book written *for* parents *by* parents to help you as much as possible as you support a loved one through self-harm and into recovery. It aims to give you some practical tips and strategies, as well as insight and information, and also to reassure you that you're not alone.

During my time working at ABC's parent helpline, I've received calls from across the UK – and also from abroad – from people of all walks of life: from mums and dads at home to those at work; from parents who are professionals as well as those in business. Some have willingly offered their experiences in answer to the questions posed in this book. These questions are some of the most frequently asked questions at ABC, although it's not possible to include everything. Your experience may not fit exactly all the scenarios that our parents have outlined, but I would encourage you to read all the questions and answers, as they contain a wealth of information and experience, giving good suggestions that you may be able to apply to your situation.

Each chapter also records emotions with which you'll be able to identify. You may find it helpful to share this book with a friend, partner, or another family member, or even with a counsellor. In the Parent to Parent sections, you'll hear how other mums and dads explain what they faced, how they felt, what they did – and I add my own recollections in each chapter. The short Did You Know? sections will provide you with some helpful facts; the Fact or Fiction? sections try to counteract the many myths and stereotypical thinking about self-harm; the Check Points provide more information, and the Action Plans are also there to guide you. All the parents mentioned in this book have seen very good outcomes; I hope this knowledge will encourage you.

Parents find self-harming shocking, especially on their first encounter. It can provoke a range of feelings, even panic. It raises many questions: What should I do? How should I react? How do we relate now to our child?

Children who self-harm find that this behaviour can place a great strain on their relationship with their parents and with other family members and friends. They can feel they are letting their parents down, upsetting them, and that their parents are constantly spying on them or nagging. Therefore the situation becomes fraught with emotions on both sides. I know this myself because when two of my daughters began to self-harm in their teenage years, we were desperate with fear and heartache. We had never experienced anything like this before and never thought we would, so it was a huge shock. As it continued, we were forced to learn about self-harming, how to gently steer our daughters towards recovery, and to discover how to support them. We also learned about the impact it had on our younger child and on our relationship as husband and wife, and about what we needed in order to cope and hold our family together. We discovered why our daughters felt the need to self-harm and we learned about injuries, wounds, treatment, and therapy. Neither of them self-harms any more. Despite the long journey towards recovery and some periods of relapse, my daughters now consider it past. So if you are facing this situation for the first time or even if you are looking for some more support and a different understanding, I hope you'll find this book helpful but, above all, that you'll be encouraged and recognize the important role you can play.

In thanking the parents who have contributed their "stories", I would also like to thank and give recognition to the thousands of parents I've spoken to over the years: for the steadfast love they have shown their children, the heartache they have experienced, the challenges they have faced, and the battles they have fought. It is to their courage and devotion that ABC dedicates this book.

Jane Smith
Director
Anorexia and Bulimia Care

CHAPTER 1

Discovering Your Child Self-Harms

Finding out that the child you love feels driven to hurt themselves in secret is very difficult to have to acknowledge and accept, and comes as a huge shock. As parents, we're not prepared for this, and may find it, at least, distasteful or, at worst, disgusting. It can also be incomprehensible and heartbreaking.

Parents often deny self-harm has happened or prefer not to know for a while. Denial is very understandable when faced with feelings and information that are too difficult to acknowledge, so if you've recently found out that your child is self-harming and you feel you simply can't deal with this, then please know that you're not alone in feeling unable to proceed. I hope that by reading this chapter and seeing how other parents have discovered self-harm (and coped with that discovery), you'll find a way of acknowledging your child's behaviour and will be encouraged to become involved and support them as they try to overcome self-harming. I believe that our support and guidance is vital and that our involvement can make a great difference in our child's recovery.

Facts about the terms for self-harm

There are many terms used to describe self-harm. Depending on which part of the world you live in, you'll hear and see it described in a variety of ways. In the UK the term "self-harming" is more commonly used, along with "self-injury" and "deliberate self-harm", although there's a debate about whether or not harming is really deliberate for all those who self-harm. Elsewhere it can be referred to as "self-inflicted violence" (SIV), "self-injurious behaviour" (SIB), "non-suicidal self-injury" (NSSI), or "self-directed violence" (SDV). There's a lack of set terminology for self-harming because diagnostic criteria don't yet exist. However, it's thought that the *Diagnostic and Statistical Manual of Mental Disorders V*, due to be published in 2013, will list self-harm as a separate disorder.

Did You Know?
Facts about the most common forms of self-harm

- *The most common forms of deliberate self-harm are self-cutting (with knives, razor blades, scissors, or even paper) and self-poisoning using tablets such as paracetamol or other harmful substances.*

- *Other forms include burning using matches, lighters or stoves; biting; hitting and pinching; and pulling out hair – most commonly from the head or eyelashes.*

- *Dragging the knees across hard, uneven surfaces, throwing the body to injure it (sometimes referred to as body bashing), and inserting objects into the body are other ways of self-harming.*

- *Self-harming doesn't always leave a mark or create a wound. Other behaviours such as deliberately using excessive alcohol or drugs, bingeing and starving, and sleep deprivation and neglect can also be used as methods to inflict harm.*

? **We've noticed some signs on our son's arms. Should we be worried?**

You might have noticed marks on your child's body – scratches, cuts, bite marks, burns, or bruises. You'll probably have questioned them about these and they might well have made an excuse. Perhaps you accepted this and then discovered more marks, *more* reasons to wonder whether they were telling you the truth. If you suspect self-harm but haven't been told, then you may also suspect that someone else is harming them – a bully or an aggressive boyfriend, girlfriend, or partner. You'll want to keep an eye out for further signs and try to find out more about your child's well-being confidentially from school or their friends, if not directly from them.

Parent to Parent

I felt such a fool, and angry with him for deceiving me as well as feeling totally naive. It was such a huge shock to find that he was harming himself. At first I thought it was just a macho teenage boy thing, perhaps even a gang ritual, or that maybe he was being picked on. I noticed the marks and asked about them but he always had an excuse. I thought he was being brave about being hurt by someone at school and I admired that, if I'm honest. I guess I preferred to believe his explanations rather than to think that he could be doing it to himself. I thought only mad people did things like that to themselves on purpose. I just couldn't get my head round it.

Steve

You may have thought about discussing your fears with someone else and maybe you've shared your worries with your partner, a close friend, or a family member. They may have dismissed your suspicions that this could be self-harm or reacted in horror, making you reluctant to share your feelings further and feeling knocked back and alone. But try to ignore their shock and lack of experience, and explain your feelings again. This may be enough for them to apologize and offer support. If you can, try to understand that their reactions reflect their lack of experience of self-harming, and try to talk to them again, explaining how you're feeling. Giving them another chance might be just what they need to apologize and begin to support you.

FACT OR FICTION?

Self-harming is a method of attention-seeking.

No! Self-harming is not an attention-seeking device. Most parents understand attention-seeking as behaviour that is deliberately chosen in order to get an immediate response, causing all attention to be focused on the child straight away. It can therefore be seen as manipulative behaviour. People who self-harm often do so as a silent cry for help with the issues underlying the self-harming. They certainly need love and care, but do not crave attention for the self-harming. Those who harm themselves do so in secret, usually on parts of the body where any marks can be kept hidden, and they are deeply ashamed of their harming behaviour.

? **Is it normal to be shocked and feel guilty on discovering self-harm?**

Many parents discover their child's self-harm quite suddenly. Perhaps you've walked in on them by mistake and found them making cuts on their skin. You may have realized they've been low in mood, but you never imagined that they could deliberately hurt themselves. Not only are you shocked and devastated but you might also feel guilty for not understanding how difficult life has become for them. However, do try not to blame yourself for anything you may have missed but think forward – about how you can support them and yourself.

Parent to Parent

We burst through the bathroom door because we were so concerned about the emotional state of our daughter. I found her sitting fully clothed in an empty bath holding her dad's razor. I was stunned and utterly terrified – so too were my other daughters. I'd never heard of self-harm, and I couldn't believe that she could ever want to do anything to herself. She was only eleven years old and had never done anything unusual before.

To realize that she was in such emotional distress was terrible. I didn't know what to do and was in a state of shock. Later, when I was a little calmer, I just sobbed out of sheer heartache. Our children are really precious to us and we love them so much. I'd spent a lifetime trying to protect her and her skin from harm, from all the care she'd needed as a baby to the little accidents that needed cuddles and plasters to sprained ankles, all of which needed my maternal nursing skills and my loving care. To think that she now purposely hurt herself was unbelievably upsetting. It also seemed to negate all the years of caring in some strange way, as if all my efforts had been wasted. Above all else I just couldn't understand why she would want to do this. I was also very scared that she might want to take her own life or that cutting herself could lead to a fatal accident. I felt I couldn't talk to anyone about this to begin with, apart from my husband, who felt just as horrified and confused as me.

We were obviously vigilant from then on. We spent time with her, trying to encourage her to talk to us about it, so we could understand it a bit better and also understand why she felt the need to do this.

Jane

If your child comes to you wanting to tell you about the distress they're feeling and their self-harming, realize that taking that step took courage. Despite your shock and sadness, you'll probably be pleased that they want to share their feelings with you and are asking for your help. Unfortunately, many parents who talk to us at ABC have discovered the self-harming, but so far their child has refused to open up about it. Parents want to know how they can approach the subject with their child.

? We think our daughter is self-harming, but she refuses to talk about it. What do we do now?

This is hard because your fears are mounting while you're feeling powerless to intervene. You may find out by coming across your child's diary, which seems to have been left out deliberately. If you're really worried that something is wrong with your child and you can't get them to talk, then it's understandable that you might glance over their diary. It's probably best, however, if you don't let them know or the trust between you might be broken. Think about whether you're the best person to approach them and if so, then engineer time together. Try not to make the issue of self-harming the first thing you talk about but enquire generally about how they're feeling and coping with life. Get the conversation going and invite them to really talk. You might find that they still don't mention the self-harming. You'll have to decide whether you'll leave this for another time or whether the moment is right to raise the subject. If you do, prepare for anger, further denial, or tears, and stay calm, offering your time, patience, and understanding. If you still feel you aren't getting anywhere then consider writing a carefully worded letter.

Parent to Parent

It was really hard not to jump straight in and accuse her of self-harming, and I needed a lot of strength and patience to bide my time for the right opportunity. I decided to take her out for a day, just the two of us, and although it was tempting to talk about the harming as soon as we'd got in the car and I'd got her to myself, I refrained. In fact we just had a good time and then on the way home I asked her if there was anything worrying her, saying that I was concerned that she didn't seem herself and was spending a lot of time alone in her room. I made sure she realized that it was OK to have private time, but that we'd noticed she wasn't around so much and we missed her. She started to relax and talk, and I thought she was about to say more, but then she clammed up and looked embarrassed. I knew it would take a bit of time. Someone had suggested writing a letter but I decided to wait a while and see if she'd confide in me another time. Thankfully she did and by this time I'd read a bit more about self-harming and felt more able to cope with what she told me. I'm really glad she did and that we were all able to get behind her.

Maggie

Check Point

Information about self-harm:

- Self-harming, although often hard to quantify, is a growing problem in the UK.[1]

- The UK has one of the highest rates of self-harm in Europe.[2]

- Those who have previously self-harmed are more likely to repeat this behaviour.

- It is possible to guide someone out of self-harming and prevent it from developing into an addictive, vicious cycle.

? Should we ignore the self-harming in the hope that it will stop? Isn't it just a passing phase?

Self-harming usually stems from deep distress and confused thoughts and emotions. It shouldn't be ignored, because your child needs help. It's essential that you listen to them and allow them to talk about it if they're prepared to, even though both they and you will find it hard. The first step in your child's recovery is for them (and you) to admit the problem, and then talk about it to someone who cares, and seek help and support. The majority of young people who gave personal testimony to a UK enquiry said that they were more likely to speak to close friends about their self-harm than to any professional or organization[3] but that families were an important source of support. It is parents who usually have to cope with the consequences of self-harm.

Parent to Parent

My partner told me I was probably imagining it and that if she was doing it deliberately that she'd grow out of it. I agreed with him that we shouldn't quiz her about it otherwise she might get attention from it and do it all the more. We both thought this was probably a teenage phase she'd naturally grow out of and that we shouldn't interfere. Looking back we weren't right to dismiss it. I decided to take her out for a day so we could talk without distractions. Once I realized how she was feeling and how stressed she was at college I told my partner that we had to support her and talk to her more about it. He couldn't accept the self-harming and was very angry with her. His approach was to tell her to stop being so stupid and pull herself together. Although she had my support, I think she needed us both to show our love and get involved. I found my partner's attitude a real let down – not just his lack of support for me as her mum but for her. I blame myself for not recognizing her distress earlier, and I blame my partner for having his head in the sand.

Kim

Check Point

Information about children who self-harm:

- Self-harming, particularly self-cutting, is common in teenagers and young adults, affecting at least one in fifteen young people.[4]

- Children with a family member who self-harms are more at risk of self-harming.

- Nearly four times as many girls as boys report self-harming.

- Studies have shown that girls often feel less able to cope with their problems; they often see their problems as more complex than they are and blame themselves; they dwell on their problems; and they use tension-reduction strategies, such as self-harm.

- Self-harming is considered rare in those under twelve, which is the average age at which self-harming begins.[5]

- Children in boarding schools, closed settings, and residential social care are more likely to self-harm.

? **We've received a phone call from school telling us that our daughter is self-harming. How should we react?**

Some parents first find out that their child has self-harmed by receiving a telephone call out of the blue from their child's school or college. The head teacher, school nurse, or tutor rings you to say that they're worried about your child. They may ask whether you knew that self-harming was going on and may even invite you in to discuss what to do. In some instances a friend of your child or their parent might contact you. In all these cases you have not only the shock but also the embarrassment of hearing it from somebody else. Unfortunately, some people first hear about it by receiving a call from paramedics or from the accident and emergency department. Your thoughts and feelings begin to accelerate until you see your child again. You don't know what to say, when to talk to them, or how to handle this very exceptional situation. Please remember that your child will probably be very worried about your reaction and very ashamed of what they've done, so do try to stay calm. However you discover self-harm, it should not be ignored, and it is vital that you try to encourage your child to talk to you or to someone else they trust. Studies show that far more young people self-harm than their parents realize or will admit to, which is very sad for all concerned. Communicating with your child on this subject may not be easy, but try to make some opportunities for them to talk to you.

Parent to Parent

At the time it was very upsetting, embarrassing, and hard to take in. The head of year rang to ask if I knew she was self-harming, because one of the parents had been in to complain. Apparently she was concerned that her daughter would learn how to do it because of my daughter. I felt protective about her and angry that she was being seen in this way when she was obviously in distress. We were asked to go into school and meet the head, school nurse, and counsellor, and although it was hard facing them all, it was a good idea as we could all decide how best to help her. I thought it was a school problem but it wasn't. She'd just finished with her boyfriend, but she thought she was pregnant and didn't think she could talk to us. Self-harming felt like a way out of her problems for a while.

Danielle

ACTION PLAN

Discovering your child self-harms

- Don't ignore self-harm if you suspect or discover it.

- Try not to accept implausible explanations in the hope that things will improve spontaneously.

- Strong emotions such as anger or disgust are understandable initial emotions, but these put up barriers between you and your child.

- Try not to lose control and completely overreact (even though that is easily done) when you first discover self-harm or are told about it.

- Think about whether there is someone else in your family who might be better suited to talk about this with them.

- Don't tell lots of people but keep your child's trust by reassuring them that you will keep their self-harm confidential.

- If they refuse to talk to you even though you suspect their self-harm, then try to guide them towards opening up, realizing that this might take time.

- Ask them about what's happening in their life and about other issues or worries rather than directing your talk at (or probing them about) self-harm.

- Don't ridicule them or be disgusted with them for their behaviour or their feelings but try to understand from their perspective.

- Do have faith that you can help them get through and overcome self-harm. If they really don't want your involvement then you can at least show your unconditional love and care.

- Don't ignore their injuries or wounds, but help them care for them.

- Remove sharp objects and tablets from view, locking these away and hiding the key. This is a recommendation of the World Health Organization.

- You can't make your home completely self-harm free, but you can help your child to avoid temptation in the early stages.

CHAPTER 2

Understanding Self-Harm

Once you have discovered that your child has self-harmed and the initial shock has subsided, you'll probably want to learn more about it to understand why they have done this. Some of us want to reach for information straight away, while others take longer to come to it. If you have been noticing marks but have feared to ask, or have been hoping things will right themselves, then making that decision to find help might not have been easy. Just to reassure you, I firmly believe that understanding something, whatever it is, makes it less fearful. We can better help someone when we know how they feel and why they feel driven to do it. Once we know more – have more insight, information, and understanding – we can also learn how to give them the best possible support to help them.

Addictive behaviour?

Although there is an addictive aspect to self-harming, not all episodes of self-injury make someone use it repeatedly long-term – in other words become a "self-harmer". My younger daughter was driven to self-harm for a brief period before abandoning it in spite of her older sister self-harming, which might have provided her with something to copy. We have parents at ABC who can confirm that self-harm can be short-lived. Therefore, if you're reading this book shortly after discovering some early attempts at self-harm, then you *can* prevent further self-injury. However, because self-harming often becomes habit-forming, most people often carry on, although not necessarily for years. I wouldn't use the term "self-harmer" for many reasons. Primarily, it defines someone by their actions in a rather disparaging way, de-personalizing them and subjecting them to a lifetime identity of self-injury. My own daughter who self-harmed for several years hated the term self-harmer, believing the way you're labelled makes you style yourself. As she was overcoming self-harm she preferred to think of herself as someone recovering from self-harm.

DID YOU KNOW?
FACTS ABOUT SELF-HARM IN ANIMALS AND HUMANS

- *Caged wild animals often self-harm due to isolation, anxiety, and frustration.*

- *Caged companion birds will pluck out their own feathers, whereas this self-harming behaviour is not seen in the wild.*

- *Self-harming is also common in mink that are bred and contained in mink farms, and by zoo animals and laboratory animals unable to engage in normal behaviours, such as the search for food and social interaction.*

- *People in highly stressful environments where there's an atmosphere of constant fear and uncertainty, such as prisoners, asylum seekers, and those in the armed forces, are more at risk of self-harm.*

What is self-harm?

Self-harm is a non-fatal self-injurious act carried out with a purpose. Self-harming is often done to provide relief and to help someone cope with a range of overwhelming thoughts, feelings, or situations. The Mental Health Foundation describes it as "causing deliberate hurt to your own body, most commonly by cutting, but also by burning, abusing drugs, alcohol or other substances".

People can self-harm for a variety of reasons: sometimes to provide pain or a lasting physical sign of distress; as a punishment for perceived failings; or to release feelings and cope with deep hurts or traumas.

People who self-harm can come to rely on it as a method of coping, using it as a way of releasing their feelings of distress in order to feel better. Sufferers often talk about the build-up of emotions such as anger, self-loathing, guilt, and panic – of being trapped by their situation as well as with their negative thoughts and feelings. Self-harming can provide relief. According to one recovered sufferer: "I used to get so wound up, so angry and full of self-loathing that I would bite myself. It became my solution somehow and certainly calmed me down, but I know it terrified my mum."

Parent to Parent

We didn't know anything about self-harm; we'd never heard about it let alone thought our child would ever do anything like that. It wasn't something we'd read about or something any of our friends had spoken of and so it was a huge shock. We were confused and frightened by it and suddenly by her. We became vulnerable and didn't know how to approach her, what to say or do, what not to say. We agonized about how to proceed; whether saying anything would make matters worse, and we had no idea how to get help. We argued together and wondered if it was something we'd done or hadn't done; if we were bad parents or had poor parenting skills. It threw us into confusion and huge sadness and because we knew nothing about self-harm we felt powerless initially to do anything at all.

Christina

FACT OR FICTION?
· · · · · · · · · · · · · · · · ·

If the self-harm is only minor, the reasons must be trivial and the feelings must be superficial.

No! The size, amount, or severity of injury does not equate to the person's depth of feelings. In other words, just because the harming may appear superficial, don't assume that your child is feeling only a little bit distressed and doesn't need your help.

❓ Don't only those with difficult backgrounds self-harm?
This is a commonly held misconception, although those who are in "closed settings" and those living together are at higher risk of self-harming. It's not only children with difficult backgrounds who self-harm, of course. Those with learning difficulties as well as those who are high achievers and perfectionists are also more at risk of using coping strategies such as self-harming and eating disorders. As a parent you may understand the vulnerability of your child, the pressures they face socially and academically, and be there ready to support them.

Parent to Parent

Our daughter suffered with Obsessive Compulsive Disorder (OCD) and we'd tried to manage it until her anxiety led into control of food. Perhaps not surprisingly she developed anorexia nervosa. During her illness she was admitted to the children's ward of a general hospital for bed-rest, tests, and medical monitoring while she was awaiting an inpatient referral. She was in a solitary room on observation for six weeks and felt at the mercy of professionals deciding her treatment. It was a terrible ordeal for us all. We were very worried about her physical state, but her emotional state was causing concern, and her feelings of hopelessness and despair were not helped by the hospital experience. The nursing staff had little experience of mental health issues and had little understanding of eating disorders. Although most of the nurses were kind enough, some openly told my daughter that she was wasting a bed and that they had really ill children to look after. That upset her greatly and she told us she scratched herself to divert some of her feelings of guilt, loneliness, and sadness. When the nursing staff saw the scratches they moved her to a private room right in front of the nurses' station in order to prevent her from self-harming. Unfortunately, they left a pair of scissors in her room. So she learned more harmful ways of hurting herself in order to handle her isolation, and hopelessness. She said that the way she was treated made her feel worthless and deserving of pain. Controlling food was in part a way of displaying protest and anger, but self-harming gave her punishment and a visible sign and reminder of her distress. We also think it was because she was cooped up alone on complete bed-rest all day every day without even the chance to walk down the ward. We her family were her only visitors, and despite our love and encouragement she felt neglected, alone, extremely depressed, and beside herself with emotions.

Richard

? Why would my daughter want to do this to herself?

Learning to accept the reasons for self-harming can be extremely hard. It is totally understandable to be shocked and stunned when first encountering it. Self-harm provides a release and a relief that the sufferer cannot experience in any other way. For some, anxiety, anger, and stress can develop into an overwhelming emotional burden; others find that loneliness and feeling isolated causes them to self-harm. So self-harm is a way of getting rid of these emotions, making the person feel calm and in control once again.

Please acknowledge, however, that it's something that needs your help, understanding, and some knowledge. With these you'll be in a better position to come to terms with the self-harming so that you can encourage your child to explain their feelings and support your child towards recovery.

Parent to Parent

I was stunned when she told me. She'd given us no problems when she was growing up and we were a normal loving family with no issues. She was a high achiever, a bit of a perfectionist, and really clever at school. She got A*s all round at GCSEs and As at A levels. She always knew she wanted to go into business and wanted to be very successful. I had some worries that she was working too hard and overdoing it when she first started her job. She worked towards promotion constantly and stayed late at the office most nights. We didn't see much of her at weekends, especially when she was promoted, as she spent a lot of time catching up on sleep. One weekend, however, she came over for lunch and said she wanted to tell us something. My mind raced as to what it could be – perhaps she'd met someone, got a raise, was leaving her job – but when she told us that she was so stressed and unhappy that she self-harmed, I was utterly speechless. She told us that cutting herself made her feel less anxious, calmer, and more in control, but I couldn't understand it. I thought it must have been accidental to start with, but no, she deliberately chose it, and what's more, she told us that she planned for it each night when she got home and that thinking about doing it helped get her through the day. My husband left the room, *which must have been very upsetting for her, but he just couldn't take it in. It took quite a lot of getting used to before I was able to understand it a bit better from her perspective so I could help support her.*

Anna

Check Point

Information about guilt:

- Initially parents may look to themselves to blame, as they often do for any issue that is affecting their child.

- Guilt and blame can take your attention away from the issues causing your child's unhappiness.

- There are many factors that contribute towards self-harming, not all to do with family or relationships.

- Remember that parents usually raise their concerns with their children long before school or NHS services are alerted and are more aware of their child's self-harm than their child realizes.

? **He says he's a failure and wants to punish himself. Is this a reason for the self-harm?**

You may recognize feelings of worthlessness and poor self-esteem in your child, which can make self-harm a form of punishment for perceived failings. Those with perfectionist tendencies can be extremely hard on themselves, thinking they're failing to meet their own high standards, and this can contribute towards self-harming. We'll look more closely at self-esteem and thinking styles as part of the underlying factors in Chapter 5. Self-harm can also be a cry of pain – a way of communicating distress to oneself and to those who care. It can act as a powerful statement to others, with the marks or scars becoming a strong and even necessary reminder of inner hurt experienced.

Parent to Parent

He was only twelve years old, just starting at secondary school and finding it difficult to fit in. He felt out of his depth with such a different style of working and very nervous about finding his way across the site. Getting to know the teachers and to feel confident in his own abilities was very hard for him.

We knew he was struggling and did everything we could to support him, but we couldn't go to school with him. He didn't want me interfering and talking to his head of year, which was understandable. We believed things would settle down and that he'd make friends and learn to cope better. Unfortunately, a group of older boys started picking on him and one of them became a real bully. My son was constantly frightened of this boy and had to take all his insults and spiteful little ways. I noticed the self-harm first as some scratches on his arm. He explained he'd gone through some brambles. I then noticed the marks were getting worse; they were red and just weren't healing. My son was angry with me for commenting and that troubled me. Then my husband was playing football with him one evening and they were mucking about in a fun but rough tackle. Our son yelped in pain as my husband held on to his arm. He brought him indoors and rolled up his sleeve. To my horror there were really deep cuts on his arm. Our son had carved a swear word in blood. He told us this was his message to the bully, his silent protest and his reminder to himself to be strong and not to be beaten.

Julia

Check Point

Family issues and self-harming:

- Many young people who talked to the *Truth Hurts – Report of the National Inquiry into Self-Harm among Young People* did suggest that difficulties in their family situations contributed to self-harm.

- They also expressed a desire for more active parenting – more love, attention, time, and care from their parents.

- A number of young people commented on serious problems at home, such as parents who abused substances, the effects of parental conflict, parental depression, separation, and divorce.

- Try to remember that many parents manage to handle illness and relationship difficulties without their children resorting to harmful behaviour.

- Indeed family members are also considered an important source of support and advice.[6]

? Is self-harming a suicide attempt?

Thankfully, the short answer is no. Self-harming is used to help someone cope, not to end life. Self-harm enables someone to express their feelings, whereas suicide stems from a desire not to feel anything any more.

Between 40 and 100 times as many adolescents have engaged in self-harming compared with those who have actually ended their own lives. The risk of serious injury and suicide is actually higher in older people who self-harm.[7] You'll be wise, however, to watch out for feelings of hopelessness and despair in your child and to be vigilant, because there is a risk that self-harm can become unintentionally fatal.

Parent to Parent

Our daughter had been very depressed, and although she'd recovered the weight she'd lost during her eating disorder, she was still struggling with life and schoolwork. We had no idea that she would do anything like this but she'd often talked about wanting to end her life, feeling she didn't deserve to live. Hearing that sort of talk and trying to encourage her was the worst experience for us, and then after one of her GCSE exams she took an overdose of paracetamol. Thankfully she told us, and her school had acted very promptly so we were able to get her to accident and emergency quickly. The staff were wonderful, caring, and very professional, which helped me feel not quite so guilty and such a bad parent, even though I knew it wasn't my fault.

She was offered an overnight stay but asked to come home as she had another exam the next day. The experience had shaken her too. After that, I could never put it out of my mind and although on the surface I seemed to cope OK, inside I was distraught. It got a bit less worrying as time went by and we had no new incidents, but I could never relax. She and I talked about it and she was really upset by what she'd done – I know it scared her. She told us she didn't want to end her life but just felt desperate at the time. She said she'd never do it again, but we found it hard not to fear for her safety each day. I always have my mobile on day and night, and if she's depressed or says bad things about herself, the possibility of her overdosing again obviously goes through my mind and I'm on alert. It does interfere with your life, not only with family but with work and with any social occasions. She calls sometimes in the middle of the night. You can't tell her not to and you can never ignore a call.

Jane

ACTION PLAN

Understanding self-harm

- Gaining some understanding about self-harm is very useful, but be aware that many of the books available are personal accounts written by people who self-harm and can be upsetting to read.

- Find opportunities to talk with your child. Spend time listening to them and try to learn why they use self-harm as a coping method.

- Try to avoid showing your distress or your emotions when letting them talk, apart from your love and care for them.

- Putting pressure on them to simply stop self-harming will probably just drive the problem underground and ruin trust and communication between you.

- Don't blackmail them into stopping self-harming on account of your feelings or those of someone else in the family.

- Try to gain understanding of any underlying issues, such as bullying, work pressures, or relationship difficulties.

- Remember that understanding why your child self-harms does not condone it, but helps them communicate some of their distress to you in a more positive way.

- Work towards helping your child identify the triggers that precipitate an episode.

- Remember the changes they're going through if they're an adolescent.

- Continue to remind them of your love even though you may be struggling to accept their self-harming behaviour.

CHAPTER 3

Adolescence and Self-Harm

As the greatest numbers of those self-harming are between twelve and eighteen years of age, we should look a little deeper to see why. Certain trigger factors and underlying causes, together with the pressures of being an adolescent today, seem to offer an explanation. Although it would be wrong to regard adolescence as the sole cause of self-harming behaviour, I believe the developmental aspect of adolescence can be overlooked. The significance of this stage of development has been lost in the public's and media's attitudes towards teenage behaviour. These attitudes generalize teenagers as "difficult". If we look more closely at what adolescence is and how it affects those going through it, then we can learn to understand why self-harming behaviour largely occurs in the adolescent years.

Adolescence – a particularly difficult time

There's no doubt that adolescence is a particularly difficult time for children – a time when they're changing and developing into adulthood. Parents are often frightened of the teenage years and back off completely from their children on the pretext of letting them have space, freedom, and control, while also admitting the fear that their children don't want to talk to them any more. Although it's often a real challenge, remember our teenagers are not independent mini-adults; they still need our involvement, guidance, and support.

DID YOU KNOW?
FACTS ABOUT THE DIFFERENT CONCERNS OF CHILDREN AND THEIR PARENTS

- *Our concerns for adolescents are quite different from their views about their own health; hence, we can often be at odds with them.*

- *Parents worry about whether their children engage in risky behaviours, including sex, drugs, smoking, and drinking, and whether they will anticipate risks.*

- *Young people, on the other hand, are concerned with appearance, exercise, sexual development, and the skills to get on with others.*

? What is adolescence?

Adolescence is a time of change from child to adult, a gradual process lasting on average three to six years. The onset of adolescence is puberty, which is becoming earlier due to better diet and increased birth weights, and can begin as young as eight years, although more commonly between twelve and thirteen. For those going through it, it can be a time of mood swings and stress, and for parents it can be a time of conflict. An adolescent is experiencing physical changes that include growth spurts, changing body shape, sexual development, and hormonal changes. You'll probably have noticed that hormonal changes usually start a couple of years before any physical changes. Children may be early or late developers and can therefore be at different stages of development at the same age, which can be hard to deal with when feeling the odd one out among their peers.

During adolescence moral thought develops, logical reasoning improves, and the ability to reflect increases. Adolescents are highly self-conscious; in fact they're egocentric[8] – quite literally believing the world revolves around them – something many a parent has been known to say! As an adolescent develops, their thinking becomes less egocentric and they begin to appreciate other people's feelings and perspectives.

Parent to Parent

I found that both my children became very difficult during their teenage years – very moody and argumentative. We were often at odds because not only had their manners disappeared, but they had little appreciation for us or what we were doing for them. I didn't know about adolescent egocentrism but I certainly understood and recognized the behaviour as rather selfish. They were both glued to their mobile phones, and when they weren't having a conversation were looking in its reflection. They seemed not to want us, spent a lot of time in their rooms, and viewed us and our life experience as sad and old-fashioned. They fought with each other a lot and it was hard for us living with their bickering. I sometimes tried humour to lighten the mood but they took exception to any teasing and got easily upset with me. My daughter asked for reassurance all the time, which was extremely wearing. When my son ever asked our opinion, he usually ignored it or told us we were wrong. My husband had many run-ins with the children because he didn't feel they were respectful. I don't think they were trying to be rude, but often they couldn't express what they were trying to say nicely and the words came out all wrong and without tact. They also got very emotional, finding it hard to control their emotions, so there were lots of tears, upset, and quite a bit of anger, particularly from our son. We hoped it would be a passing stage. My husband and I talked about their attitudes and behaviour towards us and how we would respond. It didn't always go to plan but we agreed to let many of the moments pass without taking them too personally, and we set boundaries. This meant we always corrected bad behaviour even if it resulted in a nasty retort, and after we'd corrected them we let them have the last word. We resolved never to bear grudges. We found they often apologized the next day even though it could be rather awkward and embarrassing. They knew we loved them and that we were looking out for them.

Valerie

FACT OR FICTION?

Self-harm is a problem for teenagers from troubled homes.

No! Anyone of any age can self-harm for a variety of reasons, although adolescents are more at risk of using emotion-based coping strategies such as self-harm, eating disorders, and alcohol and drug abuse. Teenagers who self-harm are from all backgrounds, many from caring, supportive families.

? **Why does she have these mood swings and emotional ups and downs?**

Adolescents are developing complex emotions as they mature, and their emotional peaks and troughs are very extreme, so they often feel out of control. During adolescence the frontal lobes of the brain that control behaviour and regulate impulsivity develop. You'll probably know only too well that adolescents are not very good at regulating their behaviour! When you realize that developmentally they really do experience problems dealing with their emotions, you can make allowances for them and your tolerance increases. Young people's intuition is still developing, which is why you'll probably find yourself forewarning them and having to explain your reactions to them, as misunderstandings are commonplace.

Parent to Parent

To be honest I thought she was being a stroppy teenager, but she was at a school she hated and where she'd been bullied. Later she told me she decided to mess about so much that she would be asked to leave. She felt she wasn't being listened to by us, her parents, or by teachers, to whom she appeared smart and stroppy. One of her friends outside of school had a freak accident and died, and it was such a shock. People at school thought she was lying and being dramatic and that affected her greatly. She began to self-harm more, but although she'd managed to hide her self-harming someone noticed the cuts on her arm and accused her in front of everyone. They said she was doing it just for attention when she just wanted to be left alone. She said, "I kicked up a fuss because I didn't trust anyone to listen to me and I misbehaved to get out. As people knew, it wasn't private any more and actually I self-harmed less." Her dad and I knew we had to talk and our relationship got a lot better. She admitted kicking up and I realized I hadn't been treating her in a very adult way, which she needed and deserved. We had long conversations and decided a goal together for the future and some changes for her schooling. I told her we mustn't ruin all the good things, which I thought was a positive thing. It mattered to her that I believed in her and listened to her when she was upset.

Diane

Check Point

Adolescent emotions and behaviour:

- Adolescents often feel very out of control as their hormones fluctuate.

- Emotional ups and downs are part of adolescence.

- Adolescents may act and react totally differently from one day to the next.

- Young people are often at different stages of development at the same age, which is very difficult for them.

- Adolescents are prone to risk-taking behaviour as their understanding of their own fallibility and longer-term consequences develops.

? **Our fifteen-year-old struggles to cope generally, so is the self-harming part of normal teenage behaviour?**

Coping is one of the key tasks of adolescence so it's not surprising that self-harming can become a coping strategy. Coping is age related, with sixteen-year-olds more likely to use emotion-focused strategies than eighteen-year-olds. Adolescence can last into the early twenties, as the brain is developing and continues to do so during this decade. Emotion-focused coping includes denying the existence of problems, and distracting away from the problem by using smoking, drinking, drugs, or self-harm to help someone feel relatively better in the short run, but of course it can be devastating in the long run to mental and physical health.

There are also differences between children of twelve and fourteen years, with older children more likely to focus on solving the problem and trying to reduce tension when faced with problems. What adolescents believe about themselves affects coping. Those who cope well have higher self-esteem; problem avoiders have lower self-esteem and confidence.

Parent to Parent

Our daughter began self-harming when she was ten or eleven. She was very mature and started puberty early, and looking back I don't think we appreciated the changes. She was badly bullied, ridiculed, and picked on by older children, which obviously affected her greatly. I was working away a lot.

My wife suffered with severe depression from the age of fifteen. She was often "up and down" and there were often periods when she wasn't "engaged". She wasn't really able to help our daughter with the bullying because she was often zoned out. It wasn't her fault and we love her but we all knew we couldn't burden her. I didn't really understand my wife's illness then, and neither did I realize how alone my daughter must have felt. She had to be "mum" to her younger brother and sister and was taking a lot of responsibility, and yet I now see that we weren't talking to her about things. We wanted to protect her and try to manage as she was our child, but she felt we underestimated her maturity and abilities. She believed that if she could cope and manage things at home, then she should have been able to share the burden. She says we should have explained the situation to her and included her. She felt alone and that she couldn't talk to anyone. Self-harming was her secret – a distraction when she was upset, frustrated, and depressed. She told me that when she was extremely worried or stressed, it cleared her mind. She said, "When you feel you have no control over things in your life you can stop life for a while and feel more in control of it. Not having solutions and finding something that might be beneficial was a potential solution for me."

Elliott

Check Point

Information about adolescent coping:

- Adolescents are more prone to substance misuse and other coping strategies that are detrimental to well-being.

- Those with good self-esteem are better equipped to cope.

- Adolescents follow the example of peers, media, and social networks in order to cope.

- Adolescents rely on friendships in order to cope with life, and these become incredibly important as they emerge from egocentrism.

- A child's individual temperament also affects the type of event regarded as being stressful, and it influences the available range of coping strategies.[9]

? My daughter is often low in mood and doesn't look after herself properly. Is there a connection between her physical health and her self-harming?

Physical and mental health are undeniably linked. Adequate and good nutrition, fresh air, sleep, exercise – all are part of the recipe for good mental and emotional stability: for mood, thinking rationally, problem solving, and coping generally. Teenagers have higher nutritional needs than any other group and yet often have the poorest diet. As their bones and muscles grow, they have an increased need for energy, protein, and almost all vitamins and minerals. However, teenagers particularly are prone to neglect some of these vital requirements, as their thinking is often immediate with little regard for longer-term consequences. So they'll often go without food or eat poorly, stay up late, sleep in with no fresh air, stay in their rooms, and not even get a walk. They're also highly at risk of alcohol and other drug misuse. Therefore, as parents we need to watch out for them and guide them. Studies show that it has become normal for young people to skip breakfast and many even skip a midday meal, choosing to snack and graze. As parents we can encourage better eating habits by eating together when possible. Eating together can provide an opportunity to chat about the day's events and for parents to find out about their adolescent's life. Although not eating with your family doesn't cause disordered eating or even a diagnosable eating disorder, parents who do provide meals for their children set a good standard for healthy eating in a sociable setting and are more quickly able to notice any food avoidance or dieting behaviour.

Parent to Parent

I tried to tell her that she would feel low if she didn't eat properly or if she stayed up most of the night talking to her friends on the phone or on Facebook. It didn't seem to make a difference and she tried to carry on her own way. She became vegetarian, which was a huge challenge for me, and then she'd find fault with what I'd prepared or wasn't there to eat it, coming home late and taking her food upstairs with her, saying she needed to work and eat at the same time. Being alone in her room wasn't good as it provided more opportunity for the self-harming. It hadn't become a serious problem but was something I was keeping an eye on. I suspected an eating disorder for a while, as I knew they were connected, but she wasn't losing weight and she definitely wasn't making herself sick. I had no idea she was drinking or smoking weed, trying to "stay in" with certain people at school. As my earlier comments had not made a difference to her, I decided to find a good moment to have a talk with her. I felt she wasn't looking after herself and was heading in the wrong direction and taking all authority away from me. We started talking about all sorts of things, and then I managed to turn the conversation round to her eating and her late nights, but decided not to mention the harming or the drugs at that time, as we would just have had a row about it. I said that I missed her company after school and that we needed a better structure to our evenings, such as eating on time and getting to bed earlier. I explained that this might help her with her grades, which was something she worried about, and that I'd be happy to increase her allowance if she could do a few things for me. These included taking the dog out after school and not using her laptop after a certain time on school nights. It wasn't bribery, more like an incentive, and it did help her focus better generally. Being home for dinner was part of the deal, and because she wasn't eating alone I noticed she ate more and became a bit more sociable. I learned more about school, her work, and her problems over the dining room table. I did notice a change in her mood, as well as her willingness to involve me a bit more. This helped us tackle her school about the bullying because it was this that made her self-harm, drink, and smoke.

Moira

ACTION PLAN

Adolescence and self-harm

- Remember the changes they're going through as an adolescent.

- Respect their space and privacy. Be careful not to take control of them or their situation, but don't leave them to their own devices.

- Develop tact and strategy when it comes to talking with them, especially about difficult issues.

- Remember that your involvement shows you care.

- Encourage your child to maintain their love and respect for you as well as develop a good and more mature relationship with you.

- Allow adolescents some freedom and let them make decisions, as long as it doesn't result in danger for them or others.

- Remember that you won't always get it right, and your well-intentioned enquiries can result in a surprising emotional response from them.

- Don't let your involvement or attempts to guide them spoil the relationship or put you off trying to communicate with them and support them further.

- Try to minimise the pressures they're under, especially with school or college work, and help support them with relationship issues.

- Don't be afraid of contacting a key member of staff to discuss any concerns you may have about your child's school or college life.

- Make time for them to talk to you and give them your attention.

- Encourage them to pursue other interests, such as sports and hobbies outside school or college.

- Build their self-esteem by praising them for their good points, not just for achievements.

- Try to recognise the difference between adolescent moodiness and a deeper unhappiness or depression.

- Continue to remind them that you love them and show affection even though you may be struggling to accept their self-harming.

CHAPTER 4

How Can Self-Harm Be Effective?

Exactly why self-harm becomes a chosen method for coping is debated and probably varies from person to person. We've seen that it can provide a way of physically expressing hurt, anger, and frustration; it can act as a release and help sufferers switch off and relax; or it can be a means of escaping difficult feelings and dealing with problems. For those who feel the need to manage their emotions immediately, self-harming provides a solution. Those who self-harm often don't understand the causes or how to escape the cycle in which they are trapped. Parents may feel they have no empathy with their child because they cannot understand why anyone would wish to repeatedly hurt themselves. That's why gaining some facts about self-harming and some insight into how sufferers feel is vital.

A way of expressing pain and turmoil

The physical expression of pain can help sufferers to validate their difficulties by providing a visual "illustration" of psychological pain or mental anguish. Self-harming may even offer an acceptable reason not to carry out obsessive or compulsive behaviour such as certain exercise regimes or habitual practices. Self-harm is, of course, also a very powerful message, and it can be a way of communicating the severity of what someone is feeling to those around them. However, not everyone who self-harms is aware of what they're doing, as explained opposite in the "Did You Know?".

Did You Know?
Facts about dissociation

- *Dissociation is often experienced by those who self-harm.*

- *Dissociation describes a psychological state in which people are able to separate themselves from what's going on around them.*

- *Those who dissociate before, during, or after self-harming are less in control of the harming. As a result, they could hurt themselves more than they intended to and they won't remember how or why they have injured themselves.*

- *It can be difficult for those who dissociate to remember or explain their self-harming, often leading parents and professionals to doubt them and conclude they must be exaggerating or seeking attention.*

? **Our daughter tells us she feels absent during episodes of self-harm and doesn't remember harming herself. Why could this be?**

Children who dissociate may feel totally detached from their bodies, or feel as if they are in a hypnotic state. They do this quite naturally when playing and creating make-believe worlds. In fact, everyone experiences dissociation to a mild degree – for example, when you go into "automatic pilot" when driving somewhere, not remembering how you got there. This "spaced out" feeling is more common when very tired or stressed. Some people develop the ability to use this state to help them to cope with overwhelming emotions or pain. To some degree this is a natural human instinct in coping with extreme situations. Dissociation helps us to cut off emotionally and to feel calm when all around feels chaotic. However, it can become problematic, especially if it's been a deep-seated method since childhood for dealing with painful and traumatic issues and if it becomes out of control. Dissociation limits self-awareness, so someone may lose track of time and may not realize where they are or what they're doing.

Parent to Parent

Our daughter was eventually diagnosed with a personality disorder and this helped us a little knowing that her condition was something recognized and experienced by others and for which there was treatment. Beforehand we were lost for an explanation of her behaviour. We couldn't understand her account of these "episodes" where she said she felt numb and absent, as if all the colour was taken out of the world and she was watching herself as a spectator. She said she had to regain her connection with reality and this is why she needed to cut herself. We still find it hard to come to terms with, and it's not something we can really identify with, as it's completely out of our experience. She's getting help now and we put the harming down to her being ill. Her consultant psychiatrist prescribed her some medication which has been very effective.

David

FACT OR FICTION?

Those who self-harm don't feel pain.

No! This isn't true, but for those in dissociative states or who have used excessive alcohol or other drugs, the pain can be numbed temporarily. The release of endorphins and increased secretions of the pain-reducing hormone cortisol during episodes of stress and pain have an analgesic effect, but the body's own pain-relieving responses don't last indefinitely.

❓ How can pain help someone feel better?

We may know and understand our children's emotions. We may also realize that for many the build-up of confusing emotions can overwhelm them. We might also know how those mixed emotions can lead to some forms of aggressive speech, violent outbursts, and a dependency on alcohol or other drugs. However, what parents usually find hard to comprehend is why cutting or burning or any other type of self-injury can physically make the person feel better. How can pain help? As well as psychological factors, there are chemical changes occurring in the body as a result of injury that cause the release of endorphins. Endorphins (chemicals produced in the brain) are released during exercise and excitement but also during pain, in order to relieve it. They have similar pain-relieving properties to morphine; indeed the word is derived from *endo* (endogenous, meaning originating within the body) and *morphine*. These endorphins have a number of uses as well as reducing pain. They help us to think more clearly and to feel calmer, more relaxed, and content. These physiological effects could be what drive the urge for some to continue to self-harm in order to manage stress and cope with pain.

Parent to Parent

Our teenage daughter told us that getting into an argument makes her upset because she's so sensitive and a perfectionist. She says she internalizes her response to arguments, believing them to be all her fault. She said, "I tend to think badly about myself. It relieves the stress and tension of it to cut myself. If you feel it's your fault you feel better for having punished yourself. Physically, beforehand I feel angry, upset, guilty, and very low, but afterwards relieved, more peaceful, and able to sleep. It's a bit like a drug in a way. It makes me feel calm, collected, that I can cope." We spent a lot of time listening to our daughter, trying to understand why she felt the need to self-harm. Eventually we began to move out of a place of shock and confusion, where all we wanted was for her to stop doing it, to a place of enquiry. We knew there had to be a better way for her to deal with her emotions and learn to think differently, but we were aware that at this stage it wouldn't happen overnight. We knew we had to acknowledge her feelings and the self-harming, though it distressed us beyond belief. We realized that if we were angry or scornful of her and this behaviour, then she would feel unable to come to us for help. So we gradually began to understand her feelings about self-harming, her reasons, and the effect that it provided for her.

Sam

? She tells us that it's important to see blood. Why could this be?

Seeing blood shocks you into reacting and wanting to care for your child, and it's hard if you find they don't want that help and wish to make themselves bleed. Blood can be a visual mark for those who self-harm, an indication of pain. The wound can be a very important sign of your child's distress, like tears, and for some, seeing blood is a necessary part of self-harming; indeed, some sufferers say they haven't self-harmed properly if they haven't drawn blood. Having dried blood on wounds enables some people to remember that they've been punished, which can help with feelings of guilt. For others, having an injury justifies acts of caring for themselves (and being cared for) that would normally make them feel guilty. The release of blood can also help people feel calmer.

Parent to Parent

We were told by the doctor to get her to draw on her skin in a red pen or to wear an elastic band on her wrist and to ping it on her skin as an alternative and less harmful way of hurting herself. We thought this was such a good idea and were completely thrown by her telling us that she had to see blood. She said it wasn't proper self-harming if she couldn't see blood, and if she couldn't then it made her feel she'd failed. Failing made her feel even more worthless, she said, and that drove her to self-harm again, so it was a dreadful vicious cycle. I couldn't understand it as it was completely opposite to my thinking. We all see blood as a warning and a sign of danger – something to be avoided – yet making herself bleed was what she wanted and needed. Blood is precious to me, so her deliberately wasting her own blood and being so unperturbed by bleeding really shocked me. I couldn't understand why she did it. I just wanted her to stop and couldn't understand why she didn't want to stop. Knowing that she was self-harming was terrible. Why would she want to do it again, when it must have been so painful? Seeing the injuries distressed me in a way I can't really put into words.

Gill

Check Point

Facts about dissociative states:

- Self-harm can be linked with dissociative states, either in inducing one or in ending one.

- The immediate pain and the need to escape from it can push someone into a dissociative state, helping them to relax and avoid the emotions they're experiencing.

- By contrast, for someone who is "stuck" in a dissociative state, self-harm can draw attention back to their physical state.

- Dissociative states are often linked with very serious self-harm, and the lack of control the individual experiences means that it's really important to get advice from your doctor.

? **I've heard that self-harming reduces someone's blood pressure. Is there any truth in this?**

The little research undertaken so far on the effects of self-harm does suggest that it reduces stress biologically. Raised levels of cortisol were found in subjects before an incident of self-harm, and seen to be lowered for several days after the incident. Cortisol is an important hormone in the body, and one of its functions is to regulate blood pressure. It is produced by the adrenal glands and is secreted in higher levels during the body's response to stress. Apart from lowering raised blood pressure, another of its effects is to lessen pain.

So self-harming may be regarded as an effective (albeit unusual) coping strategy – one that manages stress and dissociative states, helping the sufferer to gain control once more.[10]

Self-injury therefore *does* reduce stress and even pain, albeit temporarily, which could be a reason why your child might do it and become caught in its cycle.

Parent to Parent

My daughter explained her feelings this way: "I find my physical feelings build up and overwhelm me and I can't think straight. I'm in overload. I have to do something, and hurting myself gives me not only relief mentally but a physical improvement. I get to the point where I can't go on and self-harming is like pressing my reset button. Then I'm calmer, more relaxed, far less tense – able to cope and to carry on." We tried to understand and I told her there were other ways of calming herself, but she said nothing worked quite like hurting herself. I found it very hard to understand and not to be upset or angry with her but she seemed so ashamed. I figured that if she was able to accept my help then I needed to get some expert advice on what else she could do to stop self-harming, and what was driving the need.

Jonathan

Check Point

Information about how self-harm can reduce pain:

- Injury triggers the release of endorphins in order to help reduce pain.

- Endorphins prevent nerve cells from releasing more pain signals.

- Endorphins can therefore offer a physiological method of reducing difficult emotions or anxiety states.

? Our child takes risks and is very impulsive. Apart from being an adolescent, could there be other reasons?

When your child is subjected to high levels of stress, they have lowered levels of the neurotransmitter serotonin. Low levels of serotonin are linked with various kinds of impulsive behaviour and lack of constraint as well as depression; this means that they are more likely to take risks, and that it may be harder for those who already self-harm to resist the urge to do it again.[11]

Parent to Parent

We were at loggerheads. She seemed determined to do what she wanted, when she wanted, without any thought for the consequences, let alone our feelings. I was angry with her, which meant that we had rows and confrontation all the time. I tried to remain calm and work out how I was going to tackle her general behaviour before speaking to her. That provided a better atmosphere and gave her the chance to listen to our point of view and for her to have her say. Once I was in a place where I could look at what self-harming was really about, it did help me make some sense of it and I needed to get past my initial disbelief, anger, and upset and be able to be more rational. I love my daughter, and this terrifying behaviour put a huge barrier between us. I couldn't understand it so I got mad with it and her. It disturbed me having to talk about it but it did help, and it was what she needed, which was much more important. Once I understood better and we repaired the rift in our relationship, I felt we could try to overcome this together.

Janet

ACTION PLAN

How can self-harm be effective?

- Teach them how to care for their injuries with your help.

- Make sure your first aid box is kept up to date with plasters, antiseptic wipes, closure strips, and antiseptic cream for minor injuries.

- Seek medical help immediately for deep cuts and burns, overdoses, and anything else that alarms you, particularly your child's emotional state.

- Sometimes less acute or damaging forms of pain can provide an alternative to self-harm, such as elastic bands or ice cubes. Sometimes drawing on the skin with a red marker can help.

- Help your child to consider and seek professional therapeutic help. Your doctor will be able to recommend a counsellor and you'll find more help in the Useful Contacts section at the back of this book.

- Learn to recognize the build-up to an episode of self-harm and encourage your child to recognize it too.

- Talk to your child about what might help to deflect their emotions during the build-up.

- Discuss alternative methods of release, such as a punch bag, a sport, or something creative – art, music, sculpture, or writing.

- Ask your child whether they can begin to identify what might help them when the urge to self-harm strikes. This could be talking, physical comfort, sleep, or exercise.

- Don't be worried or feel rejected if your child can't rationalize their feelings or explain a lot to you, but maintain your relationship, showing love, care, and support.

CHAPTER 5

Underlying Issues

So far we've looked at how self-harming can become a mechanism for coping, both psychologically and physiologically. We've also seen how the emotions of someone struggling with self-harming play a large part. Knowing that there's good reason for your child's behaviour will hopefully help calm you and focus you. It certainly helped me to face the behaviour with less fear and panic than I had done earlier. It also helped me realize why self-harming could be effective for someone and therefore gave it some rationale. What I wanted to know next was what specifically was making *my* child react this way. What were the trigger factors and the underlying issues for her?

Issues and reasons

In order to develop a constructive and supportive approach to *your* child's self-harming you need to look more closely at why your child might be responding this way. What issues and problems might be triggering such an emotional response? You'll want to take time to listen to your child in order to learn about and understand what it is that affects them so deeply. They could be anxious or stressed for many different reasons: the pressures of school or college, relationship difficulties, their future, or the death of a loved one, to name a few. Often it's the pressures of being an adolescent and the problems associated with the physical and mental development from puberty to adulthood as discussed in Chapter 3. Perhaps we've underestimated and ignored the enormous pressure they're under.

If there *are* specific issues then you'll want to discover what those issues are and talk things over with them in the first instance. You may decide you're not the best person to talk with them and bring in someone else.

DID YOU KNOW?
FACT ABOUT YOUNG PEOPLE'S REASONS FOR SELF-HARMING

* *Young people, when asked, identified the following as causes of their self-harming: being bullied at school, not getting on with their parents, stress and worry around academic performance and examinations, parental divorce, bereavement, unwanted pregnancy, experience of abuse in early childhood (whether emotional, physical, or sexual), difficulties associated with sexuality, problems to do with race, culture, or religion, low self-esteem, and feelings of being rejected in their lives.*

❓ Our daughter has had a hard time accepting her grandpa's death and has begun self-harming. She won't talk to me. Should I be concerned?

Deep and painful traumatic events are trigger factors for self-harming. The event may be something you're well aware of and that impacts on you too, or it might be new to you and come as quite a shock. If so, you might need time to come to terms with it and to have someone to talk to. You might decide that your child would prefer talking to someone else. Try not to feel hurt or excluded but thankful that they're talking to someone. That someone might be willing to report back to you without ruining trust and confidentiality. You'll have to assess whether your child needs professional help in addition to the support of friends or family. Many teenagers and young adults refuse professional therapeutic help or agree to it but then find it hard to keep appointments, so it may be that you become sole provider and untrained counsellor whether you intended to or not.

Parent to Parent

I don't know how she found out about self-harming or how to do it, and it really came as a terrible shock, especially as she was so young. I thought she must be copying someone at school, someone very disturbed. I felt really bad that she didn't feel able to come to me and talk or that when she did I obviously hadn't helped her. The loss of my dad was really hard to bear and it affected me greatly. Maybe I didn't appreciate how hard it was for her. Of course I'd talked to her but maybe not well enough. She knew how upset I was so maybe felt she couldn't overload me with her feelings. She's a very sensitive girl and was very close to her grandpa but I think it was also about death. At her age she thought everyone would be around forever and it was her first understanding of reality. She hid her feelings and worries about me dying and about losing her granny, so she said she cut her arms to help her with the sadness. It gave her a reminder of him. Although I worried that my mum would have yet another emotional problem to deal with, she was wonderful and was keen to help. I think it helped my mum to talk about Grandpa, and it certainly helped my daughter come to terms with his loss talking about her feelings and her fears. My mum got my daughter to help her make a special garden in Grandpa's memory so she'd have a different reminder. They also made a photo album of Grandpa for my daughter to keep. Thankfully the harming did stop.

Mary

FACT OR FICTION?
· · · · · · · · · · · · · · · ·
Self-harming is a media phenomenon.

No! Self-harming is not a celebrity trend or a type of decorative body graffiti, and it's unlikely that self-harming is just a copy-cat response to media stories. However, the media (and social media) can be considered partly responsible for the rise in numbers of those self-harming. On the other hand, articles about celebrities who self-harm can contribute to greater awareness and understanding about it. There have been media reports that becoming a Goth is responsible for causing self-harm, but it's more likely that Goth or Emo culture attracts young people with issues who were therefore more likely to self-harm in the first place.

? **We know we've done nothing to cause the self-harm but why do we feel under suspicion?**

Parents often fear blame and condemnation for having caused their child to self-harm, and this is another reason why we often desperately look to find reasons. However, since there's so much misunderstanding and ignorance about self-harm, the family can be accused and parents suspected of having been abusive to their children. Sometimes parents are so emotional about the self-harming that they imagine everyone is looking at them to find fault. If you can identify with feelings of unnecessary guilt then try to keep calm and, when able, talk your feelings through with someone close to you or a professional counsellor. Abuse *is* a reason why some children self-harm but it's not the reason why *all* children self-harm. Being suspected of abuse is really hard for innocent, supportive, loving parents, and it can take courage and strength to face professionals helping your child.

Self-harming produces strong reactions. It makes some parents look to their partner, family member, teacher, or friends with suspicion, and sadly in certain cases the suspicions are confirmed.

If you suspect or know that your child is being abused then you do need to contact social care services or the police straight away in order to protect your child.

Parent to Parent

We noticed that she wore long-sleeved shirts and it was summer, so it took us a while to see the marks on her arms. She said later that she also cut her stomach. I first realized something was wrong when she didn't want to go to school and she was avoiding eating. The possibility of an eating disorder led me to have a long chat with her, and although I was terrified I tried to stay calm and to talk generally with her about what was troubling her. I was totally unprepared for her telling me that the school tennis coach had been abusing her all that summer term and was threatening her not to tell anyone.

Rachel

? What makes someone more at risk of self-harming?

Traumatic life events can be risk factors for someone self-harming. According to the NICE guidelines, life events are strongly associated with self-harm in two ways. First, there's a strong relationship between the likelihood of self-harm and the number and type of adverse events experienced. These include having suffered victimization and, in particular, sexual abuse. It's worth repeating that it is wrong to assume that all those who self-harm are victims of abuse. Second, life events, particularly relationship problems, can trigger an act of self-harm.

Risk factors that make someone more likely to self-harm include mental illness, certain disorders (including personality disorders, eating disorders, anxiety and emotional disorders), depression, and drug, alcohol, and substance abuse. It can be extremely complex and without a single cause. A family history of self-harming also contributes. Children with a learning difficulty and those in care are also more at risk of self-harming. In addition, emotional factors, including past traumas and the memory of them, are also found to contribute. The thought processes and styles of thinking of those who self-injure also play a big part.

Parent to Parent

I've struggled with depression all my life and until five years ago was an alcoholic. I can say it now and I can tell you the exact number of months, days, and hours since I stopped drinking. When I drank I didn't know what I was doing. It numbed my feelings and helped me cope but it had a terrible effect on my children. I'd had a hard time growing up and had been in care for a while and I didn't have much support. I thought it would be so different when I had kids of my own but the depression got in the way. I know they had to grow up so fast because I wasn't there to help them. I'm sure they never saw me cut myself, but perhaps the drinking showed them a form of self-harm. Maybe they noticed some marks. I was devastated when I found my daughter self-harmed. I don't think self-harming is something you inherit, but maybe the depression and need to cope is linked with personality. It certainly seems to run in my family. Now that I'm not drinking, I see things differently. I try to support my children and talk to them. I have a community psychiatric nurse who's part of the Crisis Team and I can ring them when things get on top of me again. My husband has been amazing, so too my children. I just wish things had been different.

Roz

Check Point

Information about self-esteem:

- Nowadays there seems to be a trend to confuse self-esteem with self-confidence.

- Self-esteem is how we think about ourselves as individuals – how we value ourselves – whereas self-confidence is our ability to do something, to perform a task.

- Many people with good self-esteem still struggle with self-confidence to a degree.

- We tend to associate low self-esteem with not having been held in high regard as a child, but this is not always the case.

- Many children have low self-esteem despite the affirmation and encouragement given to them by their parents.

？ Our daughter suffers with high anxiety and she self-harms. Does anxiety contribute to self-harming?

We all experience anxiety occasionally as it's an emotion that plays an important role in adapting our behaviour in response to risk or danger; however, for some, anxiety can become a serious, even overwhelming, problem. Anxiety has real consequences for physical health as well as for emotions. Apart from causing chest pains, palpitations, panic attacks, shaking, nausea, trouble concentrating or sleeping, headaches, and migraines, it can give rise to self-harming. Anxiety is also associated with more mental health conditions than any other emotion. At the severe end of the scale it can develop into phobias and anxiety-based disorders such as Food Avoidance Emotional Disorder and Obsessive Compulsive Disorder (OCD). Eating disorders are driven by anxiety, and the full titles of anorexia *nervosa* and bulimia *nervosa* show that these are anxiety-related conditions.

Parent to Parent

One of my daughters developed Obsessive Compulsive Disorder when she was young. The further anxiety she experienced when her sister was desperately ill in hospital caused her to develop an eating disorder as a way of coping. I first recognized anxiety when she was very young. She became very upset if anyone got into trouble at school and found it hard not to imagine that she'd been responsible. It was quite illogical and we tried humour to get her out of it. Making mistakes was something that she was really afraid of and therefore school and homework were always fraught with emotion. We learned to be careful not to make critical comments, but her friends did, and so there were a lot of relationship problems. I thought she was just a very deep thinker and that she over-analysed everything but I never imagined that her anxiety would grow out of control. She developed a hand-washing problem because she feared passing germs to those she loved most, thinking they'd become ill. We couldn't reason with her so we considered professional help for the anxiety and its effects on her life. As the eating disorder developed at this time we were forced to find that help quickly.

Caroline

Check Point

Information about self-hatred:

- Children with perfectionist tendencies often berate themselves if they "fail".

- Even if parents have never pressured their children, some will label themselves "useless", "a failure", "fat", or "stupid".

- Self-hatred can be the result of someone not meeting their expectations in academic work, of failing to achieve in sport or relationships, or even of not having the body type they want.

- Self-hatred can be a trigger for self-harm.

? **We wonder whether our child struggles with depression. Could this have caused her self-harming and what should we look out for?**

Depression is one of the risk factors of self-harm that you'll probably be most aware of, as your child's low mood is hard to hide. You'll experience them being withdrawn, unusually quiet, and tearful, having lost their sparkle, humour, and usual outlook. You may find them withdrawing from hobbies, activities, and relationships, appearing listless, lacking in energy or drive. You may find them talking darkly and hopelessly as well as having extreme mood swings. One minute your child can be very fragile, needing your love and encouragement, and the next minute they're arguing with you, shouting, being aggressive, and refusing to listen to reason. You'll know deep down that this is not just typical teenage behaviour but is symptomatic of negative thinking and feeling low. Regular low mood and depression is deep-seated and enduring, so can't be confused with a phase or a regularly occurring episode such as PMS or PMT. Some children even talk of wanting to end life, of seeing no way out of their difficulties, and this should always be taken seriously because hopelessness is a major cause of fatal self-harming.

Parent to Parent

My daughter struggled with depression and turned to self-harming as a way of managing her mood. The depression exaggerated her difficulties, making the harming more appealing to her. Once she had self-harmed she found that it didn't really change anything; it was just a temporary relief, and in fact the shame and the marks made her more depressed, as she was so worried about what people would think of her or say to her. It depressed her that now she was also unable to go swimming, which was the sport she liked most, and this contributed to her feeling isolated, which of course made her feel more depressed. It was a dreadful cycle of misery and unhappiness for her and for us all. Our doctor suggested antidepressants, and although I wasn't keen to begin with, I realized that the medication would hopefully lift her mood and give her a better, more level playing field for life, so we all thought we should give it a go.

Dan

ACTION PLAN

Underlying issues

- Try to keep calm when talking with your child.

- Remember how difficult it can be for them to express their feelings and rationalize their behaviour.

- Give them time to open up without prompting them or jumping in.

- Really listen to them.

- Encourage further dialogue and communication between you.

- Try not to focus on the self-harming but rather the reasons behind it.

- Try to learn something of why your child feels compelled to self-harm.

- Try to help them to identify and discuss any problems they are facing.

- Encourage your child to believe that they can find solutions and other ways of coping and that you will help them, working with them, not taking control away from them.

- If the reasons for your child's self-harming are traumatic or you feel out of your depth, you'll need to obtain trained professional counselling either through your doctor, the Child and Adolescent Mental Health Services (CAMHS), or privately, from an accredited counsellor or counselling organization (see Useful Contacts).

- Do consider getting some help and support for yourself as you come to terms with this very upsetting and demanding behaviour.

CHAPTER 6

Predisposing Factors

As well as the issues causing someone to self-harm, there are other factors thought to make someone more likely to do it. Indeed, the same issues and events often exist for many children and can affect them equally. Some of them turn to self-harm while others do not, so why are some children driven to respond by self-harming? What predisposes them? It's thought that a genetic influence in terms of personality is partly responsible, and how people think about themselves and their situations can predispose them towards self-harming behaviour, making them more at risk. Research shows that thinking styles affect the ability to solve problems, and poor communication skills contribute to the use of detrimental coping strategies. The event or issue might be the tip of the iceberg, but the predisposing factors are the hidden part of the problem and also need addressing.

Patterns of thinking

Research tells us that certain patterns of thinking are strongly linked with negative emotions, depression, stress, and anxiety. Low self-esteem has a profound effect on people because of the way it affects their thinking, their perception of themselves, and their relationship with others. A traumatic event can trigger negative patterns of thought, and these can develop into powerful cycles of behaviour. One of the most well-known forms of professional psychotherapy is cognitive behavioural therapy (CBT), which helps someone to identify their thoughts and feelings and to relate their thinking to their behaviour in order to make changes. We'll look at this therapy and others in more detail in Chapter 12.

DID YOU KNOW?
FACTS ABOUT NEGATIVE STYLES OF THINKING

- *Certain styles of negative thinking exaggerate emotions such as anger, anxiety, panic, and helplessness.*

- *The thinking fuels the emotions that lead to self-harm, so the way people think really is an important part of the cycle of self-harm.*

- *Most of us experience some of these ways of thinking from time to time. However, those who find themselves thinking negatively most of the time are more at risk of harming themselves.*

? Our daughter's anxiety around problems and her inability to find solutions causes her to self-harm. Is this usual?

Learning to cope and to problem solve are part of adolescence, and in many ways all young people are learners at this time of their lives. However, some children seem slow to develop good problem-solving abilities. It could be that they haven't been shown how to solve a problem or that when they've tried they've been criticized or ridiculed, so they associate the task with defeat and give up. Maybe they've had little past experience of problems, or you've always sorted things out for them, or you as parents have difficulties problem solving. Maybe your child struggles to problem solve because of a learning difficulty or an inability to communicate their thoughts about a specific problem. The way someone thinks greatly affects the ability to solve a problem, and if someone is in a highly emotional state with a lot of anxiety, then thinking rationally without panic can be very hard for them.

Parent to Parent

We found that our daughter got easily upset and confused. She had difficulty putting her thoughts in order when speaking, often getting tongue-tied and fearful. She also had problems when writing. English comprehension exercises were particularly difficult for her, as she couldn't remember which part of the text she'd read and found extracting the relevant answer almost impossible. When she started in the senior school she felt more pressure of work and became more sensitive to the opinions of her peers. We discovered that she was hurting herself, and although we were really surprised and upset, we appreciated the struggle she was having. Hardly any of her teachers realized that she got so uptight about language work and that her self-esteem was declining. We also began to realize that she had significant memory lapses and forgot even the simplest thing. Sometimes she admitted to believing that she was somewhere else, somewhere calm and peaceful. She'd always been a bit dizzy and forgetful, and as she was growing up it was more obvious, probably because she had to be more self-sufficient at senior school. She had more to remember and the teachers didn't make allowances for her. Thankfully, one of her teachers thought our daughter might be dyslexic and that the school could request an educational psychology assessment. We hoped it might explain why she felt the need to hurt herself. We had to wait a long time to see the psychologist, but when we did we were surprised and somewhat relieved to find that our daughter had a learning difficulty. She was on the autistic spectrum, with language-processing and short-term memory problems. She

*wasn't dyslexic and in fact her reading age was high
enough, but she needed extra tuition, more support,
and time allowances for her work and exams. We also
realized that she needed extra sleep because trying
to remember and process everything made her very
tired. We began to see a reduction in the number of
times she self-harmed once she realized that we, and
people at school, were taking her seriously, listening
to her, and recognizing her difficulties.*

Jane

FACT OR FICTION?
. . . .
***All those who self-harm are depressed, which is
easily overcome.***

*No! However, many people who struggle with self-
harm do suffer with depression. Those who suffer from
depression often voice negative thoughts repeatedly,
which requires constant careful handling; so caring for
someone is hard. Depression doesn't always have a
cause and therefore is not necessarily reactive. It's not
usually a passing phase, and you may need to consider
medication for your child to help them manage the
depression to reduce the risk of self-harm, so do seek
medical advice.*

? **She always puts herself down despite all our praise and
affirmation. What can we do?**

If your child thinks in this way they are generally very hard on
themselves, seeing only the bad in themselves and their lives. They
struggle with self-esteem and put themselves down. They seem to
refuse to listen to your praise and affirmation for any achievements
or talents, explaining it away or arguing against it. Those with
perfectionist tendencies and those who suffer with depression are

particularly prone to think like this. Telling your child they should be grateful for all the good in their lives makes them feel guilty, so instead, keep on praising your child and reminding them of their positive attributes.

Parent to Parent

Yes, of course we all have times of being a bit low or down. Usually, though, there's a cause and one works through it, pretty swiftly in our house. We had seen some bleak and turbulent teenage times when my elder son was going through his mid-teens. During that time, everything we said seemed wrong and he communicated only by grunting and door slamming. But during our daughter's eating disorder years, it was on a different scale altogether.

The depression fuelled the illness, and the barrage of self-hatred was so hard to withstand because it was constant and it seemed as if nothing we said made any difference. All our logic, our encouragement, our considerable efforts to motivate her and get her involved with things, and the praise we gave her were either ignored or thrown back at us. It wore us down over the many months and we didn't know how to respond and go forward.

Richard

Check Point

Types of negative thinking:

- self-deprecating thinking;

- pessimistic thinking;

- black and white thinking;

- jumping to conclusions;

- assuming the thoughts of others;

- obsessive and compulsive thinking.

? **We think he's being typically moody and pessimistic for his age and this will pass. Are we right?**

When someone is very sceptical about good outcomes they'll believe that the glass is always half-empty rather than half-full. Although many adolescents experience mood swings with some emotional lows, this could be a style of thought that is linked with depression, sadness, and loneliness. You might well find your child recalling and dwelling on the negative and projecting that negativity into the future. So, although their day might have been mixed, if they're pessimistic they'll only remember the things that went wrong and assume that all their days will be the same. Trying to encourage your child to think positively and to remember the good is important, but you'll probably find the task very draining. As with many of these negative patterns of thought, you might need to approach your child's doctor and discuss possible treatment options.

Parent to Parent

Nothing was ever right – nothing we said or anyone else said – and listening to him express these views was hard to take. Listening to him arguing and hearing him talk so bleakly made me boil over. He seemed ungrateful and sullen and appeared to wallow in misery when he had so much to be thankful for. Reminding him of this didn't make any difference. We tried challenging his dark outlook on life but it didn't change how he saw everything. I hadn't thought that he might be depressed, and I didn't really like the thought of him going on medication because I worried that he'd be hooked on it for life. I went on my own to see my doctor to discuss him in private, and he said that if I could bring him in, say, for his next asthma check, then he'd talk to him and maybe recommend a course of antidepressants, especially as our son was also deliberately hurting himself in all his misery. I feel bad that we didn't think about depression earlier, but we didn't think he had anything to be depressed about. It took us a while to realize that his depression wasn't caused by any incident. We have a few older family members with depression so we wonder if it is genetic.

Meg

? **Why does our daughter always leap to wild conclusions?**
Someone struggling with this kind of negative thinking jumps from the initial thought to something far more negative and catastrophic. To parents this seems wild and illogical. Stress and anxiety fuel this thinking, and if your child is struggling, they'll experience a loss of control, which in turn leads to more panic. Although what they say can even sound slightly comical, for the child – and for you their parents – it's very upsetting and draining, especially when it is expressed frequently, as is often the case.

Parent to Parent

Our daughter got very upset about her academic achievements. She was a worrier who had high anxiety and a real fear of failure during her younger years. We noticed that she tended to react very illogically and emotionally, for instance if she did badly in an essay or exam. Instead of being able to feel simply disappointed if she received a worse mark than expected, she wasn't able to contain this disappointment or easily forget it. Her thinking became exaggerated and her critical thoughts gathered momentum. Sometimes she would express some of the thoughts along the way, but often she'd jump from A to Z, leaving out the staged thinking in between. She'd start with saying, "The essay is bad", which would jump to "I'm useless at writing essays", "I shouldn't be doing the subject", "I may as well give up the course now", "I'll fail the exam", "I'll never amount to anything", "I'll never get a job or be happy ever." Sometimes she'd leap completely from A to Z and just conclude that the essay was bad and in despair say, "I'll never get a job." We couldn't laugh it off with her, as we found she got all wound up and more likely to self-harm when she voiced these negative and very destructive thoughts.

Nigel

Check Point

Information about negative thinking:

- Black and white thinking often results when someone is very rigid in their opinions.

- A child who thinks negatively is unable to see the range of possible explanations and instead views things in terms of one of two possibilities: good or bad, success or failure, right or wrong.

- Those who think in extremes like this are more prone to depression and self-harming.

- Helping someone to look for the "grey" by suggesting other views and possibilities is really useful, even though you may need to do this over and over again.

? She often gets upset with me because she assumes what I'm thinking. What should I do?

You might recognize your child telling you what you're thinking without even asking you. They assume you'll think badly of them or you're disappointed in them. They may even say, "I know what you think of me" or "You hate me, don't you?" They expect a negative reaction and can even become paranoid thinking that others are always critical of them or hold them in low regard. This style of thinking causes someone to become very introspective and nervous, and it can make your child lose confidence, isolating themselves from others so as not to risk imagined judgment or condemnation. You'll be looking out for social withdrawal and helping your child to realize that they can't know the mind of others; that their feelings aren't based on fact, but on supposition and assumptions. It may seem as if you're not getting anywhere with them, but constantly helping to correct their assumptions, pointing out that they cannot know your thoughts as they're yours and yours alone, will hopefully pay off.

Parent to Parent

We battled on with great difficulty. We found we could get little rest from the endless self-hatred and arguing and her need for attention – reassurance as well as cuddles. She would argue with us about her size repeatedly so that eventually we learned to stop it. Instead of the "Yes, I am!", "No, you aren't!" pantomime, we found that if we gave her our opinion it meant that she couldn't tell us that we were wrong – they were our opinions. So, one of us would say, "Well, I don't think you're all the things you say about yourself, even if you think them." If she tried to argue with that we would say, "No, that's not what I think and you can't know what I think," and that would end the argument.

We were surprised and very relieved to hear the consultant say that she thought our daughter would benefit from some antidepressants, as she felt that her depression and high anxiety should have been resolved by normal eating for the past eight months. She said it was likely that the anxiety and depression had pre-existed before the onset of the eating disorder.

Richard

ACTION PLAN

Predisposing factors

- Keep in mind that negative thinking can fuel episodes of self-harm.

- Help someone who expresses negative thoughts to see the other possibilities.

- Try to understand the impact that negative thinking patterns have on behaviour.

- Look out for the build-up of emotions that results from negative thinking and try to deflect your child from harm.

- Don't try to joke about their distress or blame them for being ungrateful.

- Consider going to see your doctor to discuss your child's thinking and/or behaviour.

- Have a think about whether other members of your family suffer with depression or negative thinking.

- If you have other children, keep an eye out for them adopting similar ways of coping with distress.

- Consider therapy and antidepressants for your child.

- Keep on praising your child and reminding them of their positive attributes.

- Since the way someone thinks greatly affects their ability to solve a problem, help your child untangle their thinking and take more logical steps towards a conclusion.

- Talk to their school or college in confidence about the emotional struggles your child is having.

- Someone at their school or college may help your child with problem solving and help them communicate and articulate their thinking.

CHAPTER 7

Self-Harm and Eating Disorders

Some experts regard an eating disorder as a form of self-harm, even though the harmful effects on the body are felt slightly later on. However some eating disorder sufferers do actively seek the immediate pain that purging and starving provides. That pain and the psychological expression of it can provide a powerful statement to the sufferer: "When I was upset and wound up, I couldn't eat. If I was annoyed with my mum, my dad, or my family, I'll admit to thinking, 'Well, I won't eat then.' I felt I couldn't eat but it also served to punish them. Of course it also hurt me and became a terrifying vicious cycle I couldn't get out of."

Working on ABC's helplines over the years I've seen just how often the more usual forms of self-harming (cutting and paracetamol overdosing) co-exist with an eating disorder so that self-harming becomes almost symptomatic of one. Poor body image and disordered eating are associated with suicidal behaviour in girls,[12] and those with eating disorders are twenty times more likely to attempt suicide than someone without. The acute mental strain produced by an eating disorder makes someone more at risk of self-injurious behaviour. Many of the risk factors for someone self-harming apply equally to eating disorders. Anxiety fuels an eating disorder and is also a strong contributory factor for self-harming. The negative thinking styles of those driven to self-harm also exist for those who develop eating disorders. The underlying issues and trigger factors for self-harm are often the same for those with eating disorders: stress, family breakdown, grief, bullying, and abuse.

What is an eating disorder?

An eating disorder is another method of coping that creates more problems than it solves. What might begin as a child's means of coping with their feelings to make them feel more in control develops into a powerful psychiatric condition in which their eating and relationship with food becomes driven by their emotions. An eating disorder also produces a range of physical difficulties and health problems, such as restlessness, problems with sleeping, depression, and the inability to think clearly. For those who develop severe anorexia nervosa with extreme weight loss, there are a number of serious physical risks, including osteoporosis, lack of periods and fertility problems, chest pains and palpitations, even heart attacks. Eating disorders are life-threatening and life-limiting, causing more deaths in those under eighteen years than any other mental health condition; therefore, it's vital to consult your doctor if you suspect your child is developing an eating disorder.

DID YOU KNOW?
FACTS ABOUT EATING DISORDERS

- *The American Diagnostic and Statistical Manual of Mental Disorders provides the diagnostic criteria for eating disorders.*[13] *There are three main categories at present: anorexia nervosa, bulimia nervosa, and EDNOS (Eating Disorders Not Otherwise Specified). It is possible for sufferers to develop an eating disorder that crosses the boundaries of the separate diagnostic criteria and therefore contains some or even many of the features of other eating disorders. For more information, see* The Parent's Guide to Eating Disorders.

- *Eating disorders can appear to start with body hatred and an overwhelming need to be thinner. However, they actually often start as anxiety or emotional responses to bereavement, bullying, illness, divorce and separation, redundancy, depression, or abuse.*

- *Low self-esteem as well as low self-confidence can often be found at the root of an eating disorder, and a genetic predisposition in terms of personality is thought to exist. Certain styles and patterns of thinking such as perfectionism, black and white thinking, and extremely negative thinking can also contribute to the development of an eating disorder.*

? Should my child be losing weight?

Unless your child is overweight and on a medically supervised diet, weight loss is a sign that something is not right. Children are still growing until the age of sixteen and should not be losing weight. They should be gaining weight every three months irrespective of any height increase, for which even more weight gain is required. Please remember that boys can also develop eating disorders, and twenty-five per cent of those affected at school age are now male. Those in the teenage years are particularly at risk, but someone of any age can develop an eating disorder. Any weight loss in a developing child needs investigating by a doctor, and you'll want to make it as easy as possible for them to speak to their doctor, perhaps by going with them, writing to the doctor in advance, or making a list of the points you both want to cover. If you suspect your child is developing an eating disorder, then do contact ABC for advice (details are given in the Useful Contacts section at the back of the book).

The weight of someone with bulimia nervosa is usually normal, so it can be harder to spot. They have the same need to restrict eating and also think highly critically of themselves and their bodies. For some reason not fully understood, their control breaks down, so they find that they binge on foods they consider forbidden. Being sick is a method of purging (or getting rid of) the food eaten or the feeling of it in their stomachs. Anorexia nervosa can be a non-purging or a purging type – in other words, some people can lose a lot of weight and also make themselves sick. Other purging methods include laxative abuse, compulsive exercise and over-exercise, diuretics, and slimming pills.

Parent to Parent

We put it down to his age and his hormones to begin with, but then a few people started to comment on how he was becoming a tall thin streak and my sister asked me if I thought he was losing weight. I felt bad because I hadn't noticed. Perhaps it's harder to see when someone's with you every day, and because my sister hadn't seen him for a while, she'd seen the change in him.

It was good to be able to talk it over with her because she's one of my best friends and she asked me some good questions that got me thinking. What was his eating like? Did I know how much he weighed? Did I know how much weight he'd lost? What weight should he be for his age and height? Was he unhappy? Being bullied? Things like that. I didn't know the answer to many of them and together we decided to do some finding out, without alarming him. Once I knew what I was looking for, it was a bit easier, but still awful. I noticed that he'd play with his food and I found food on the underside of the plate when I took it for washing up. There were even bits of food under the table.

I decided to serve up only his really favourite meals and see if he was off those. I began to watch him when he had his friends round to see if he was having crisps and things with them and to see whether he was eating normally, having no problem snacking. I also wanted to know if he was just filling up before meals as well.

Once I knew that he was deliberately avoiding food I knew I had to find out his weight and see whether he had lost any weight. I contacted the school nurse to see if she had a record of his weight, because my niece's school weighs their pupils each term. Sadly my son's school didn't. The nurse suggested having him go to our surgery nurse to get weighed on the pretext of his tiredness or his asthma check that was now due. In the meantime, we were advised to find out how many calories he needed each day for his age and to be firm with food, trying harder not to let him get away with not eating. This was difficult, but the alternative was to let him carry on losing weight, which we couldn't do.

Sue

FACT OR FICTION?
. . . .

An eating disorder is a devious method to manipulate others.

No! It's not about manipulating others. It's another private method of coping. Those struggling with eating disorders are not able to snap out of it and suddenly eat normally. Many sufferers, although highly intelligent, cannot apply reasoning and logic to their eating, as they've become phobic about food and are unable to eat normally again or to view themselves in the mirror as they actually are.

? **How do I recognize signs of an eating disorder, and whom should I alert?**

Parents are often the first to spot the signs of an eating problem. You'll notice that your child's relationship with food or their behaviour around food is starting to change. Avoiding food, making excuses about eating at home, and avoiding eating at home or out with friends, are telltale signs of a possible eating disorder. It can often be hard to know whether your child is eating their lunch if they're at school, college, or work, but you can ask one of their friends or teachers to be discreetly watchful and keep your concerns confidential. You may have to insist that your child's school monitors them during lunch, maintaining that your child's case is a special one, just as those with food allergies would be. Many schools and colleges are pleased to be alerted to a possible problem your child may have with food and are discreetly vigilant, providing a very useful contact for information and support for you both. Skipping breakfast, avoiding lunch at school or college, cutting out snacks, refusing certain foods or food groups, reducing portion sizes, exercising obsessively, or *suddenly* becoming vegetarian or wheat or lactose intolerant are signs that something is not right and needs checking out.

Parent to Parent

We asked her why her packed lunch was returning home some days and she gave good enough reasons. She said she'd been late for lunch so didn't have time to eat it all, or she hadn't liked the lunch I had given her. When I prepared other food for her she had other excuses. In addition, she wasn't sleeping well and complained of being cold all the time, often wearing baggy clothes and extra jumpers to keep warm (which I later realized also hid her shape and size). She wouldn't talk about eating or what was going on and so I asked her teacher to do some discreet investigating. It was really tempting for me to ask her friends and their families and quiz everybody, but I'd been advised to tell as few people as possible to avoid antagonizing my daughter and making her feel that everybody was talking about her. It was hard enough trying to find out what was going on with her, and I didn't want to drive the problem underground.

Jane

Check Point

Signs that your child might be developing an eating disorder:

- a change in mood – sadness, depression, anger, withdrawal, tearfulness;

- tactics and excuses to avoid eating;

- dieting or refusing certain foods, such as fats, carbohydrates, and snacks;

- stress, anxiety, pressure from work or school coupled with a changing attitude towards food or eating;

- friendship and relationship problems in addition to a changing attitude towards food or eating;

- perfectionism and obsession with achievement;

- addiction to sports and exercise, over-exercising;

- complaining of stomach aches and feeling full;

- low self-esteem, body hatred, and self-hatred.

? **We're noticing a change in her behaviour generally, as well as difficulties around eating. Is this significant?**

Apart from an altered relationship with food and eating, a child who's developing an eating disorder will usually show signs of depression, withdrawal, and mood swings that are unusual, even for teenagers. You might notice your child becoming more timid and clingy, almost regressing in age, or you may find a noticeable anger and hostility. Often it is both of these at different times. Since an eating disorder is a coping strategy, when confronted by parents or professionals your child will probably act defensively. This reaction is due to the fear that the strategy they rely on is threatened. Of course, being malnourished or underweight will affect the mind, and you'll probably notice your child's mood is low, they're emotional and unable to concentrate for long, or they have difficulty making choices. The use of alcohol, and the subsequent withdrawal, can exacerbate depression. Self-harming often results from the low feelings that a child experiences when they stop using alcohol.

Omega-3 Fats and Carbohydrates are important for guarding against depression. A diet rich in these increases levels of serotonin in the brain, which is thought to improve mood. This may be one reason why people with depression often increase their intake of carbohydrates during bad spells.[14]

Parent to Parent

She lacked energy, which I put down to sadness and the fact that now she was only comfortable eating a few items of food, so clearly she lacked essential nourishment. She'd go into a terrible rage if I tried to get her to eat her normal range of food. As her eating deteriorated she developed more extreme episodes of self-harming. These took the form of gouging her cheeks with her fingernails and hitting her head repeatedly with her fists right there in front of me, and the force of these blows caused her to cry out in pain. Shocked doesn't describe it. I felt wounded too, emotionally scarred by it and also detached from my life somehow and from decency. These severe attacks came at odd moments, so weren't predictable, although the worst period was when she was at stage 2 of the re-feeding process[15] and was in response to eating more than she felt comfortable with. Then there was what I later understood to be "body bashing", where she would throw herself down the stairs in order to harm herself. That was incredibly shocking, so too the compulsion to do it over and over again and to find that trying to comfort her or calm her had little effect. We had to restrain her and hold her while the episodes passed, and when over, to help her see to her injuries. We were wrung out with the worry and emotions ourselves and felt there was no one we could turn to because they'd have been even more shocked and would possibly have judged us, which we couldn't have taken.

Jane

Check Point

Signs of an active eating disorder:

- weight loss, unless on a medically instructed or supervised diet;

- lethargy, tiredness, but not sleeping well at night;

- constantly feeling cold, and trying to keep warm with baths/showers;

- wearing clothes that are too big or having to buy clothes a size or two smaller than normal;

- hair loss or hair lacking lustre, growth of fine body hair, particularly on backbone or arms;

- periods stopping or failing to start at puberty;

- frequently visiting the bathroom directly after meals;

- signs of vomiting, including raw knuckles, sore throat, or swollen salivary glands.

? **I'm pretty sure my child has an eating disorder. What should I do?**

It can be difficult not to panic and fear the worst, so it's good to get some initial advice and the opportunity to sound out not only your concerns but also to evaluate your child's behaviour around food.

You could be reassured or be given the support to seek further professional help. It's better to do some reading and research and to speak to a helpline or your doctor than to deny the problem or hope that it might just go away on its own. Try not to confront your child and get angry with them about their eating, but see if you can get them to open up about what might be triggering the disorder. Are you able to provide a listening ear, or is there someone else they might prefer to talk to who could liaise with you without breaking confidence? If your child is an adult living away from home then your involvement will be a little more difficult. You might be able to guide them towards thinking about the pros and cons of their eating disorder and support them while they contemplate change, albeit from further afar. Once you realize an eating disorder is developing you'll also need to help stop any weight loss and food avoidance and find them some medical and therapeutic help. You may need to persuade them to seek that help, take them to sessions, and even take part.

Parent to Parent

Her anorexia was like quicksand: the deeper she got with it, the more difficult it was for her to think her way out. Her brain was obviously being starved of adequate nutrition and she was far less rational, far more hopeless as she lost more weight. She self-harmed because the lower her weight dropped, the more depressed and hopeless she became. She said she didn't really know why she did it. There was no real reason, just that she felt so bad about herself and somehow it seemed to help. We tried to stem the loss of weight by being quite firm at mealtimes and providing meals cooked to a calorie quota. We eventually persuaded her to see our doctor who referred her for specialist help.

Emily

ACTION PLAN

Self-harm and eating disorders

- If you think there's something wrong, there probably is, so trust your instincts. Admit the problem to yourself and get help and advice early.

- Try to piece things together. Try not to panic but get as much information as you can from a few significant people in order to build up an understanding of the situation.

- If your child is still at school or college, let the relevant staff know what's happening and ask for information.

- If mealtimes are becoming fraught, try to calm things down and take some pressure off all those at the table.

- Continue to provide normal meals for them and insist as firmly as you can without coming to blows that they eat these.

- Plan to see your doctor alone or with your partner to discuss your suspicions and to learn the approach your doctor would take.

- Consider your own attitude towards food and exercise. If you're dieting or talking about it, are you inadvertently giving your child the wrong messages?

- Don't ignore weight loss, particularly in a child, because they should be gaining weight as they grow. Weight loss needs investigating by a doctor.

- Find out how much weight your child is losing by weighing them (or having them weighed) weekly if they live at home.

- Encourage them to talk to you or somebody else they trust about their difficulties.

- Build trust by keeping their confidence.

- Show unconditional love, support, and understanding despite their behaviour and irrational tendencies.

- Don't rile or provoke your child into further arguments, as this will put up barriers and halt communication.

- Try not to criticize, give orders, or attempt to "fix" them.

- Don't comment on their appearance or mindset; for example, "You look like a stick insect" or "Are you mad?"

- Don't blackmail them, saying things like, "Look how you've upset your sister/spoilt family life."

- Get more information and support for yourselves as parents.

- Encourage them to get help from a doctor, or take them and reassure them about going.

CHAPTER 8

Coping with Self-Harm

Most parents find there is a host of demands on their time: going to work, looking after children or caring for an elderly grandparent, and keeping the household running. In many cases both parents work and come home tired after a long day. When a child is struggling with any issue, particularly if it's damaging and unresolved, your emotions run high on top of all the other pressures, so it's important to get some help, some rest, and take your mind off self-harm from time to time. Living with self-harm and having to care for and support a loved one day in, day out is exhausting. I found that in order to cope I had to prioritize things and overlook some tasks that were less important so I could manage those which were really necessary. I also had to look seriously at relaxation and how I could help reduce my own tension.

Coping with your feelings

Learning to cope with self-harm means looking at how to deal with the emotional aspects of the self-harm (and *your* emotional responses and behaviour too) as well as the physical consequences of your child's self-harming. Coping with your own emotions is really important, and hopefully by now your understanding about self-injury will help to equip you to move forward. It's good to identify and accept your feelings. You may experience anger, shock, distaste, blame, guilt, sorrow, anxiety, panic, helplessness, and hopelessness, among other feelings. Dealing with your emotions includes not only identifying your feelings and understanding them but also learning to overcome your shock, disguising your feelings when being around your child, and staying calm. However, that *doesn't* mean bottling up your feelings forever, and in fact you really do need to find outlets for them. You could choose a trusted friend with whom to talk, or perhaps your partner or a trained professional, such as a counsellor. You'll benefit from some non-verbal therapy as well. Relaxation is important, and if, as it does for me, the word conjures up images of a couch, candles, and mood music, then think again! Relaxation involves many kinds of stress-reduction techniques that should be *regularly* undertaken. It could be listening to music, singing, reading a magazine, sitting in the sun, breathing deeply, dozing, having a bath, going out for a walk, enjoying a sport, painting, doing some gardening, or going for a swim. We'll be looking at the part relaxation plays for those struggling to overcome self-harm, but it's vital not to overlook your own stress load as well and take some action.

DID YOU KNOW?
FACTS ABOUT STRESS

- *If you experience continual worry and anxiety, you'll notice the effects on your health, such as not sleeping enough or at all, headaches and migraines, indigestion and stomach aches, IBS, chest pains, and raised blood pressure.*

- *Stress is the body's response to too much pressure and anxiety.*

- *The worry you have about your child's self-harm affects you physically as well as mentally, and there's a knock-on effect for the rest of your family.*

? How do we cope with the worry, anger, and all the rows we're having?

Holding on to emotion means that when it's released it can spill out as anger. We often don't mean to be angry, but remember that our children can't understand our thinking and recognize the resulting emotions. They see you're angry with them when actually you're worried sick. You do need to offload your worries and talk them through with someone whose opinion you trust. If you have a partner, then share this considerable problem with them, for it's so much better having both of you in agreement, supporting each other. Next, try to work on relaxation and to anticipate those situations that trigger angry reactions from you.

Parent to Parent

The worry about her and my inability to help her made me ill. We were often at screaming pitch about her self-harming, and it was just so exhausting arguing with her and trying not to upset my other children. The rows often happened at the end of the day when we were all tired. She later said that she'd feel emotional and tense and would misinterpret what I'd say or how I appeared, and because I was tired and had been worrying about her all day having had little sleep, I know I didn't put things across so well and was much less tolerant than I should have been. All these things made her more defiant and cling to her destructive way of coping. Learning how to relax was important for me and it helped our relationship. It also helped my relationship with my partner, which was suffering as well. I learned some good relaxation techniques and made myself go out for walks to get some fresh air. I often found I had a new perspective when I came back, and because I was fortunate not to be out at work, I was also able to take a nap after lunch. I had thought I was being indulgent but my doctor told me that it was good for me and that my blood pressure had come down as a result.

Melanie

FACT OR FICTION?
• • • • • • • • • • • • • • •
It's only the child who self-harms who needs help.

No! Siblings are not immune to self-harm. They often struggle to cope when their brother or sister self-harms. Apart from being frightened by the harming (and remember that sometimes they may witness it or see the injuries), they can feel that family life is out of control. When your attention is so focused on the child who self-harms it's not surprising that siblings can often feel neglected. You'll want to be sensitive to their feelings to support them too. Watch out for them showing signs of unhappiness, withdrawal, unnecessary guilt, problem behaviour at school or college, difficulty coping, and even loss of appetite.

? **What can I do to cope better with her self-harming?**

Coping with self-harm involves you trying to understand your child's behaviour from *their* perspective, feeling *able* to cope and getting to a place of some acceptance. This doesn't mean you approve of their behaviour but that while you're working towards recovery, you don't condemn the behaviour and alienate them. Don't think you necessarily need to have all the answers; in fact, sometimes it's best to say that you're not sure how to help and to ask them what *they'd* find most useful. Young people interviewed for the National Inquiry into Self-Harm identified being listened to with respect as a key factor in recovery. As you listen to your child you'll recognize their deeper feelings in their panic, confusion, and distress, and you'll try to understand what underlies their anger, self-loathing, anxiety, and turmoil. While this process is gathering strength, try to keep communication open and let them know that not only will you be there for them but also you still love them the same and nothing can come between you. It's really important for your child to know and feel this unconditional love and for your other children to witness this too and feel secure. If your child refuses to discuss their self-harming or doesn't appear to want to take any steps towards changing their behaviour, don't despair. If you have a good relationship with them and can contain your distress, you can gently guide them to open up about their self-harming. Do remember the shame that surrounds self-harming and the difficulties adolescents have trying to put their thoughts and feelings into words.

Parent to Parent

When I first knew what he was doing I couldn't raise the subject with him, because I was disgusted by it and angry with him. I knew that spending time listening to him was important, but it wasn't always possible with everything else going on in the house – a meal to get, homework to supervise, picking up my other son from judo or the gym. When we did have an opportunity to talk he'd often be in a foul mood and yell at me to leave him alone. So then I wondered whether he really did want to talk and I suppose I was grateful for being off the hook, 'cause I don't know how I'd have reacted to what he was telling me. I was scared of what I might learn and that I'd feel out of my depth ... just wouldn't know how to help him. My husband agreed to start the conversations with him and actually broach the subject of self-harming, because we knew we couldn't just ignore it, hoping it would go away by itself. Taking my son to football on a Saturday gave my husband a good opportunity to spend more time with him and to chat about all sorts of things on the way back home. Even when the team had lost we found our son was more able to talk rather than just get angry or sullen. This also helped me with my anxiety because it shared the load, and we were seeing some improvements, which was hopeful.

Bev

? If self-harming is a short-term solution, then does it mean it only lasts a short time?

Self-harming, like many coping strategies, is indeed a short-term solution using short-term thinking. That doesn't mean that the self-harming will last only a short time but that the person struggling can only see their immediate problems (not the wider context) and that they reach for a quick solution without looking at the long-term consequences. This ability to take a long-term view develops as people mature, and that's why short-term thinking can be associated with adolescence. If you can, help your child to think further ahead than their immediate struggles and therefore to think about the scarring that might occur or the stares and reactions of others. At the same time help them to remember their positive attributes, their talents and abilities (some of which, you can remind them, can be used to help them eventually overcome the self-harming), and the good things to look forward to in the future – a holiday, their next step in education, or their career. Reminding them of all that is positive can help them think a little more widely and reaffirm them. Inevitably you'll have times when your efforts are rejected, but try not to take this personally. In my experience, encouragement is also about timing, and we can't always get the timing right!

Remember that when we talk to our children, they do hear what we say, even though they may not appear to have taken it in. Don't forget that a letter or email can be an effective way of communicating, enabling us to choose our words carefully and calmly and to deliver what we'd like to say without the emotions or expressions of a face-to-face encounter.

Parent to Parent

To begin with I couldn't get her to talk about why she hurt herself. Although I knew what she was doing because her teacher had spoken to me, she still refused to see there was anything wrong and continued to dismiss it. She was in denial and I felt powerless to help. I tried asking other members of the family if they would speak to her but that didn't work. She just got angrier and screamed at us, saying that we were all ganging up on her, that there was nothing wrong; it was all in our heads and we were all making a fuss about nothing, making her feel worse. So I backed off and thought I'd have to wait until things deteriorated – a major accident maybe or her teacher telling me that she'd broken down at school or worse. It put a horrible strain on me and my relationship with everyone in the family. I was out of my mind with worry and devastated that she was rejecting my offers of help. I felt I had to tread on eggshells with her and pretend. We were angry that we seemed to have had our parental authority taken away from us and were on the back foot, waiting for her to invite us in when it suited her. I felt really helpless to know how to go forward. I did make an appointment to see my doctor to get some advice and just have someone to talk to, and that was quite helpful. He arranged some counselling for me, and although it didn't help her come forward for help, it did make me feel more in control of my emotions and responses, which certainly helped our relationship and the atmosphere in the house. We never really got to the bottom of why she self-harmed, but as time went on she certainly seemed more able to share what was happening in her life.

Kay

Check Point

Relaxation for you:

- Although coping with a child who self-harms is extremely stressful and upsetting, you can help control your emotions and help manage your own stress by many different methods of relaxation.

- Relaxation includes breathing deeply, getting fresh air, exercising, and sleeping.

- Try not to abandon all hobbies and interests, because physical or creative activities can be really beneficial for your emotional health.

- Many people find that talking through their problems and their feelings with a friend, family member, doctor, or counsellor helps them relax and manage anxiety.

? My child is unable to see this as a problem and do something about it. Why won't she talk about stopping self-harming?

One of the reasons why we find it so hard to get our child past denial of self-harming to a place where it can be talked about and suggestions for help accepted, is due to the stages of psychological contemplation. With any decision (and attempts) to change behaviour, especially destructive ways of coping (such as smoking, alcohol dependency, or self-harm), a process begins that involves several stages. The first stage is denial, or pre-contemplation. At this stage the person refuses to admit to themselves (and others) that there's a problem and can be adamant that nothing is wrong or needs to change. Caring for someone at this stage is very hard, and carers need to be encouraged to help guide their loved one to the next stage – contemplation – where the ability to think about the situation, and some pros and cons of the behaviour begins. This stage can take a considerable length of time, as the person will be more receptive to change on some days than on others. Therefore it can seem as if there's one step forward and two steps back – to denial. After contemplation is the stage of decision, and then action, where a commitment to change takes place and the person concerned is actively trying to apply changes, often with the help of others.

Parent to Parent

I found that my daughter went to and fro many times within the early stages of contemplation: she began to mention small negative thoughts about the self-harming and yet carried on using it as a coping strategy and defending her need for it. She seemed to argue about it with herself and was starting to look a little further ahead, opening up the channels of communication. Therefore I found I could gently add a few tactful comments or ask her a question, which eventually led to her asking for my help. She began to consider a point in the future, this time next year or after college or five years' time, all of which were markers for whether she'd still be self-harming and how she and others would view it. She found writing these thoughts down in a private diary very useful.

Helen

ACTION PLAN

Coping with self-harm

- Try to identify what emotions you're feeling, perhaps writing them down and explaining why these are justifiable responses. This will help you make sense of your feelings and see the load you're carrying.

- Ask yourself whether you could express your feelings in other ways.

- Talk about your feelings with a trusted friend, your doctor, or a counsellor.

- Seek help for any physical symptoms of stress you may be showing, such as raised blood pressure, insomnia, chest pains, stomach aches, panic attacks, and depression.

- Give yourself permission to relax and unwind.

- Consider what types of relaxation work for you and try to do at least one each day.

- Prioritize chores and work commitments to allow some time for yourself.

- If necessary, take some time off work if possible.

- Accept offers of practical help from your friends and family.

- Allow yourself to cry, shout, and get rid of any anger, frustration, and sadness somewhere private.

- Do set some boundaries for your child's behaviour. You may tolerate certain behaviour while they're struggling with self-harming, but that doesn't mean that they have permission to do or say anything they like.

- Explain to any other children and close family that your child is going through a difficult time, without giving details. Of course if your other children witness the self-harming or any rows surrounding it, then you'll need to explain it to them.

- Beware of betraying the confidence of your child in your need for help and understanding.

- Do lean on your partner or spouse, because as parents you're in this together. In the event of separation or divorce, don't be afraid to contact the child's father/mother, even if they live some distance away.

CHAPTER 9

Moving Towards Recovery

It's really important to believe that your child can eventually overcome self-harming and to see recovery as a process rather than an event. Remember that recovery is about progress (and also some backward steps) and therefore develops over time. In order for your child to progress they need a good foundation and preparation. As a parent you can offer significant help, playing a large and vital role in the recovery process. Your child will be discovering as well as needing motivation and encouragement. They'll also be learning new strategies, which as they move forward will reduce their dependency on self-harm.

Please remember that the foundation for recovery is about developing a strong supportive relationship and open lines of communication so that you can encourage your child to think about their self-harming and talk about their issues. If they're not at a stage where they can talk about self-harm or indeed want to make some changes, then you'll be limited in the help you can give. Building their self-esteem, helping them with their emotions, helping them develop alternative ways of coping, encouraging them when thinking negatively or critically, looking together at their problems, and helping them to problem solve are all steps towards recovery. We'll examine each in a little more detail in the rest of the chapter.

Moving forward

If you have their trust and have developed good control of your own emotions then you'll be in a good position to help them consider their self-harming. You'll need to help them recognize their feelings, to consider the pros and cons of their behaviour, and to identify key factors. You'll also need to have hope, and firm belief, that together you can eventually come to a place of sustained recovery. Try not to take control of them and their situation. If you can, talk with them and plan steps together. This could be first recognizing the triggers to their self-harming, then considering the build-up of emotion, and then looking at ways of reducing the number of occasions and severity of the harming by learning alternative coping strategies.

DID YOU KNOW?
FACTS ABOUT UK CHILDREN'S VIEWS ON RECOVERY

- *Over a quarter of children interviewed in The Mental Health Foundation's* Truth Hurts *enquiry stated that having someone who would listen to them, giving advice and support, was key to their recovery.*

- *Students from Asian backgrounds were particularly likely to say that being listened to would be useful in helping them to cope and to avoid turning to self-harm.*

- *Girls were more likely than boys to emphasize the importance of talking, listening, and receiving advice.*

- *Participants were three times more likely to suggest talking to friends or family members than to mention mental health professionals or drop-in centres.*[16]

? **How do we encourage alternative ways of coping?**
Just concentrating on stopping the self-harm shouldn't be your aim, even though it's an understandable thought when you first encounter it. A "zero tolerance" approach would not only be very hard to implement but would also make your child feel

they've failed you and let themselves down. It would reduce the opportunity for them to come to you for help and might therefore encourage the harming to continue in secret. Your main task involves helping your child to discuss and use different coping strategies, maybe with the help of a professional counsellor. Learning and developing these strategies is very important, for without them the harming will remain as the principal way of coping. Some of these strategies will be ones that reduce anxiety, such as those that calm or self-soothe. Not everyone develops adequate or successful methods of self-soothing but these can be taught (see Check Point: Ways of helping your child to relax p. 114); however, you'll be wise to discuss methods when your child is not at the height of their distress. Other alternative coping strategies include learning to identify emotions and the build-up of feelings, and practising expressing thoughts and emotions verbally, or channelling them in different and safer ways.

Parent to Parent

It was the most shocking and upsetting thing, but apart from wanting her to change, I knew that I had to alter my approach and give her some space and privacy, because she said I treated her like a prisoner. It was hard because I imagined her cutting herself whenever she was alone in her room, but I managed to stay calm so we could talk. I heard how she felt about how I responded to her. She also saw it from my side a little and agreed to come and tell me if she felt the need to harm, to get out of her bedroom and talk or do something else like watch the telly with her brother, or take the dog for a walk – anything that calmed her, diverted her attention, and brought her out from being alone. She said it helped, as it delayed the harming, and then after a few months she said she didn't do it so often, felt less wound up, and not as much in need of it. We felt she was learning to calm herself and learning to control the urges to self-harm. We promised not to go on about it all the time, and we carefully engineered more time together, less time for brooding.

Nicola

FACT OR FICTION?
. . . .

Is teaching children to cut themselves safely and to care for their wounds the solution?

Some experts, including those who contributed to the NICE guidelines for self-harm, recommend parents give children information about how to cut cleanly and sensibly to avoid arteries and explain to them how to treat the wound and avoid infection. This is often referred to as harm minimization. Even when this advice is appropriate it's only a part of managing self-harm rather than part of recovery. Please remember that harm minimization advice isn't suitable for those who self-poison, and therefore any attempts at substance misuse or overdose should always be treated professionally as soon as possible after the harming has occurred. If your child takes any harmful substance, even if it's a cry for help, then you should call an ambulance immediately or drive them to Accident and Emergency if that's faster, since speed is essential to safeguard life.

? How can we help her reduce anxiety, as it seems to drive the self-harm?

There are many different ways of reducing anxiety, and your child may find some more helpful than others. Learning how and when to use some of these suggested strategies takes time; therefore, replacing self-harm will not happen overnight. Apart from encouraging them to use relaxation techniques, you could help them address the issues causing anxiety. If it's a problem that can be solved, then your child might welcome the opportunity to think it through with you and come up with a plan. If it's something that can't be sorted until later, then having a sequence of steps to take and an advance warning of any likely feelings can help them reduce anxious thoughts, even feelings of panic.

Thought blocking is a method of taking the mind off the subject causing anxiety by visualizing it being boxed up or pressing a stop button to end the repetitive thoughts. I found this a very useful strategy for helping my daughter with the compulsive, repetitive, anxious thoughts of her OCD. She also benefited from having someone to gently correct her negative thoughts and inner dialogue (self-talk) and gradually learn a new, more positive, one.

Parent to Parent

At first I couldn't see a way forward. Knowing and thinking about the self-injury made me really anxious for her safety; whether she was at school or at home, I felt there was no break from the threat of it. To stop her doing it (which is what I felt I should do), I followed her everywhere at home. Even her little sister had begun to hide all the sharp knives. If I was with her, I reasoned, she wouldn't harm, but it made us row all the time, was very stressful for me, and was impossible to keep up. She felt suffocated and more anxious, which she said made her want to hurt herself even more. It's easier to see it when you step back but when you're in the situation it's fresh and painful – you can't see a way out, you do what you think is best, and are led by your emotions. I talked to my doctor and he suggested we all try to help her manage her anxiety, first of all by getting her to do some sport in the fresh air. He thought this might also help with the anger she felt, and he also suggested hypnotherapy to enable her to feel more in control over her emotions.

Sonia

? Can she learn to reduce the number of episodes of self-harm? How can we help?

This phase can be lengthy but is all part of the recovery process. Encourage your child to take small, manageable steps, learning first to extend the period between acts of self-harm by getting them to do something else to delay the harming.

You'll need to have knowledge and understanding of the events and emotions that trigger your child's urge to self-harm, and also recognize the build-up towards an episode of self-harming, spotting the signs of tension. The build-up can act as a warning to you and them once they've learned to understand their triggers. Appreciating warning signs means recognizing your child's mounting emotions, situations that may cause them difficulty, and knowing the most "at risk" times of the day. When you're more accustomed to their triggers, you'll be better prepared to prevent their emotional build-up leading to self-harm.

Parent to Parent

Although I wanted him to stop the harming straight away, I began to realize that it would take time to wean himself off the dependency – a bit like anyone addicted to certain behaviours. As much as I wanted self-harm out of our house, I had to go at his pace. We had a good relationship and he did confide in me; therefore, I used this to steer him towards overcoming and enabling him to recognize times of strain and stress that caused him to self-harm. He found the harming always worse at the end of the day and also on days when his workload overwhelmed him. We also realized he was more likely to kick off and almost engineer a row so he could justify self-harming. He began to see a pattern emerging and realized he was caught in a cycle, but with our help it was one he could learn to change. Harming wasn't inevitable, as he'd previously thought.

Mike

Check Point

Ways of helping your child to relax:

- listening to music;

- taking time out to get fresh air;

- walking, running, dancing, or other exercise;

- playing a sport or doing another hobby;

- taking a bath;

- reading a magazine;

- drawing, painting, sculpture, and crafts;

- writing down thoughts and keeping a diary;

- sleeping or taking a nap.

? How can school or college help our child as they begin their recovery?

There are a number of issues and situations that produce high stress and anxiety for those who turn to self-injury. These include relationship difficulties and school, work, or college pressures. Girls were found to be particularly affected by exams and other school pressures, and by teachers who did not intervene effectively in bullying. Many pupils describe the damaging effects of bullying in their schools, wishing for more effective handling. There is something you can do to help them cope and reduce pressure from the source. Ask your child if they would like your direct involvement and then begin to think who would be best to contact. Is it their tutor, the head, or a teacher whom your child best relates to? Of course you might want to talk directly to a member of staff in confidence without your child knowing, and this is probably easier if they're young and you don't need their permission.

If your child is at boarding school and using self-harm as a way of coping with life, then you'll probably need to make the head of house, matron, or school nurse aware. Although this is a difficult conversation to have, they really do need to know, as they have a duty of care to your child, acting *in loco parentis*. You may not wish to talk about the self-harming on your first approach but begin by seeking information about whether your child is happy there, managing work, getting along with friends, appearing at lessons, and handing work in on time. Are they managing expectations with regard to exam grades or feeling overwhelmed? You could make an appointment to see a teacher and discuss your child. You might find they agree to accompany you and talk directly to your child about the issues they're having and why they're not coping.

Parent to Parent

We knew that on certain evenings our son needed more discreet supervision, more care and opportunity to be around us – not alone where the temptation to resort to self-harming was greater, something which had become a habit. The self-harm was definitely worse during the evenings and on days when he felt most tired and overwhelmed. We had to look out for this. I did speak to his tutors with his permission, not about the self-harming, which he wanted to keep private, but about giving him some free periods in the timetable. The combination of several small changes to his workload and us helping him with his thinking generally, and about the self-harming and its negative aspects, did contribute to his recovery, although it seemed mighty slow at the time and was a terrible ordeal for us all.

David

Check Point

Helpful actions from your child's school or college:

- Teachers can be made aware that your child is struggling and oversee your child's well-being.

- Teachers can arrange free periods in the timetable, put them in a different set, allow them to change subjects, and provide extra tuition.

- Your school will probably be able to provide counselling support. It's worth pursuing this because according to pupils who self-harmed, a counsellor was considered more helpful than a teacher.

- Having a contact at the school who understands your situation and is supportive of your child can be vital to you and to your child's recovery.

- The flexibility and understanding that a school can provide can be really important in keeping your child in education, as well as giving them some breathing space.

- Support from school can make a big difference to managing self-harm along the road to recovery.

? **What are replacement techniques?**

Sometimes referred to as distraction techniques, these are things that replace the harming with alternative forms of pain. You can suggest your child holds ice cubes for short periods or tries flicking a rubber band on their wrist. For those who especially need to see blood, then using red dyes or red markers can be worth trying. Ripping up a telephone directory or using a punch bag can reduce anger or tension, so too can a physical sport, but not at the height of distress. The success of these techniques seems to vary with the age of the child, and the severity and duration of the self-harming. Suggesting some of these techniques may offend the person who self-harms, so you would be wise to consider carefully whether any of these might be appropriate and when.

Parent to Parent

It was once she'd begun to think about her life with self-harming and see a kind of overview of herself with the misery of being caught in its grip – only then could she consider talking to me, whom she trusted not to freak out by then. It was a combination of my being calm, wanting to help and support her, and her being at a place where she wanted to try to harm less. She said, "Saying to myself that I wanted to try to harm less was much more achievable than saying I was never going to harm again, which I knew I'd fail trying. I did get to know the start of a build-up, and instead of just going with it as an inevitability I told myself to do something else, like go downstairs and watch an episode of Friends *or hang out with my sister rather than be alone." This really helped her get over the urge if she'd caught it early enough. Of course there were times when it all went wrong and she got over-tired and so emotional she just needed to self-harm. This did make her feel she'd failed, but we both agreed not to let it put her off trying. She said she couldn't have done this in the early days and really needed the understanding that her family gave her and the motivation to harm less. She and I were able talk about the future and she got to think about the scars she was getting and what it would be like to be stared at all the time, but she definitely wouldn't have been able to think like this or think at all rationally in the early days.*

Jo

ACTION PLAN

Moving towards recovery

- Keep talking to your child and encourage them to say how they're feeling and coping generally, rather than just quizzing them about the issue of their harming.

- Ask yourself whether you could approach the subject of self-harming in a different way.

- Find out what support they need and see what you can offer. Is it listening, more time with them, more space for them, sharing their problems, or showing them more fully that you're interested in their life without taking over and appearing too controlling?

- Suggest or arrange for your child to enjoy some relaxing or alternative pursuits.

- If you know they're struggling with a school-related issue, then speak to their tutor, although you may need to discuss this first with your child.

- Recognize the build-up towards an episode of self-harm and encourage them to do the same.

- Gently encourage them to think about some of the factors that increase the likelihood of self-harming, such as consuming alcohol, not eating enough or regularly enough, or not having sufficient sleep.

- Remind them of their good qualities, their self-worth, and your love.

- Work with them, maybe with the help of a counsellor, to help channel and reduce feelings of anxiety, frustration, and confusion.

- Explain to other family members without betraying your child's confidence that they need some special attention, careful handling, space, and quiet time. It can be useful to explain this to younger siblings, who can, without realizing, contribute to tension and invade privacy.

- Help your child to think of other things they can do when they're feeling mounting pressure and the urge to self-harm. This could be choosing company, going to sleep, going for a walk, or talking to you.

- Don't be afraid of talking about any wound your child may have made and showing your concern.

- Don't be afraid to talk about the dangers that come about by burning or cutting and to explain how to minimize risk.

- Don't keep paracetamol or pain-relieving drugs in the house unless they're locked away, and try to be vigilant if your child has money to buy them.

- Explain the dangers of drug overdose and say that they can always come to you or ring you in times of emergency. Reassure them in advance that you will never be angry with them or dismissive.

- Keep your mobile on twenty-four hours a day and arrange cover when you're busy or need a break.

CHAPTER 10

Managing the Physical Effects of Self-Harm

Although you'll be very concerned about any damage your child has inflicted on their body, there are often several obstacles to overcome first in order to allow you to help them. As self-harming is a secret strategy, they may not want you to see any injury because they're embarrassed or frightened of how you'll react. Have a think about your reactions and your methods of communicating. Will you be able to stay calm when seeing any injury? If they refuse to show you, then how could you open up the dialogue between you? Do you feel you could enquire generally about self-harm, talk about wound care, or even comment with tact and kindness if you notice a burn or cut? Children who self-harm often do so on parts of the body that will be less noticeable – below the pant line or on the calves, inner thigh, or inside of the arms – so that you might have little idea it's going on, let alone know how to intervene. Your child may feel they can't talk to you or tell you if they're hurting, more so if you show little sympathy, tolerance, or appear angry. If your child is an adult not living at home, then it is more difficult to know about their injuries. Rather than asking them directly, you could consider asking your child's friend, partner, or another relative (a sibling perhaps) whether they know about your child's self-harming. Thinking about how you'd approach someone, choosing a good time and place, practising your opening words, and maybe writing them a letter are all worth considering.

Self-poisoning

Damage caused by overdosing on tablets can be harder to spot and also to anticipate, as these can be bought, hoarded, and taken without you noticing. Keep a lookout for depression, low mood, and any dark or suicidal thoughts being voiced and don't ignore them. If your child tells you they've taken something, whether liquids or tablets, then do take this very seriously. Ask them what they've taken and get them to an emergency department, or ring for an ambulance if that's quicker, making sure their airways are kept open. You should not try to make your child vomit but call the emergency services. If your child talks of hopelessness and not wanting to carry on, then find out whether they've done anything to hurt themselves. If in doubt arrange an emergency examination. If your child is telling you this by phone, then make sure someone else is with them or can get to them quickly, tell them to wait for you, and drop everything to get there yourself. Everything may turn out fine but the alternative could be far worse than a wasted journey.

DID YOU KNOW?
VITAL INFORMATION ABOUT SELF-POISONING

- *Irreversible liver damage can occur within three days of taking a paracetamol overdose. Being malnourished, at low weight, or using alcohol increases the risk. Therefore, it's absolutely vital to get your child to an emergency department or call the emergency services if quicker.*

- *Get information from your child about any poisoning substances used and tell the emergency doctor on arrival at the emergency department.*

- *If your child can't or won't tell you what they've taken, look around for empty containers and give these to the paramedics or doctors at the emergency department.*

? How can I get my child to see a doctor for their injuries?
Although many injuries are managed at home with a good enough knowledge of first aid, even minor wounds can become infected, requiring professional examination and a prescription for antibiotics. You may find that your child refuses to see the doctor, and you'll have to decide whether you can manage the wounds at home or whether they really should see a medical professional, in which case you might need to persuade them to go. If your child is over sixteen years, they have full confidentiality and the right to decide whether or not to see a doctor or receive treatment. You can make things easier for them by offering to take them and go in with them, or you can write a note together for the doctor ahead of the visit. Choosing the doctor best able to deal with emotional health is a good start. You may persuade your child by explaining that the doctor needs only to examine their injury and maybe to prescribe medication. Many people who self-harm fear being judged, criticized, forced to accept psychotherapeutic treatment, or even admitted to hospital, and these fears can escalate into real panic and a refusal to see a doctor. Focusing on the medical help only and reassuring your child that the self-harm doesn't need investigating at this stage is a good way of calming them and persuading them to see a doctor. You may feel that your child needs further support by the doctor and a referral to more specialist mental health services, but where there's time this should be done slowly and carefully, with the consent of the sufferer and acceptance of treatment.

Parent to Parent

I felt awful when her injury became infected, because I'd been so appalled by her admitting the self-harm that I hadn't asked her about any sore places; I'd ignored that side of things. I just couldn't go there. When she told me that her teacher had arranged for her doctor's appointment, I felt hurt at being left out but more ashamed that I'd let her down. It should have been me who cared for her and I let her go it alone. I became much more able to accept my responsibility for caring for her wounds after this, and she seemed grateful of my interest and concern. She didn't resist seeing the doctor together, although she asked me not to talk about the reasons for her self-harming, avoiding it until she got to know him better. I guess she wanted to see whether he'd be sympathetic and trustworthy; to consider whether he'd be someone she'd ask to help. That was hard for me because I needed to tell him everything, but I respected her wishes, and a few sessions later she did start to ask for help with the harming rather than just for the injuries.

Jane

FACT OR FICTION?

People who self-harm like to show off their scars.

No! People who self-harm are usually very conscious of any scarring that occurs and do not invite comments or welcome stares, instead keeping any scars hidden. Although some people consider their scars a sign of previous distress or of having triumphed over events and issues, this acceptance often takes considerable time and support.

? How should I treat the cuts she makes?

Clean, close, cover, and check are the main points here. You'll need to treat a wound quickly and carefully to help it heal well and to minimize scarring. First, make sure there's no object in the wound, removing it carefully if possible, and then clean the area to avoid infection. If the wound is superficial then cover with a sterile dressing, otherwise seek the opinion of a health professional as to whether or not stitches (or sutures) are required. If an embedded object is large or not easily removable then leave it there and apply firm pressure to both sides of the embedded object and seek immediate professional help to remove the object, clean the wound, close it with sutures or surgical glue, and dress it.

If your child has a deeper cut, then hold the flesh together, keeping it closed with self-closure strips, and cover with a sterile dressing. Don't use antiseptic creams on skin you need to bring together, or self-closure strips won't adhere. Keep an eye on the wound, re-dressing it occasionally, watching out for signs of infection as well as good healing. Signs of infection include angry red skin, which may ooze pus and swell, accompanied by a fever.

If you're seeing significant blood loss, particularly after ten minutes of continual pressure, then you'll need to get medical help. In the meantime continue to apply direct pressure to the wound with a clean cloth or with clean fingers (ideally using disposable gloves) until a sterile dressing is available. If the injury is to a limb, raise it and support it. Once bandaged, if bleeding seeps through the dressing, then cover it with a second bandage. If you notice bleeding continues to seep through this, then remove it and reapply a fresh one. Paramedics and emergency departments may use surgical glue to close the wound, and stitches may be required; if so these need to be applied in the first twenty-four hours after the initial cut.

Parent to Parent

Our daughter used a razor and then just blades to harm herself, usually on the inside of her lower calves. She didn't often ask for help treating them, although I know that sometimes these were very sore when she showered or took a bath. At the start of her period of self-harming I found it hard to look at the marks she made because it was so upsetting, and also I don't manage blood very easily without feeling sick, but I had to toughen up because one evening she came downstairs looking very white and shaky. I sat her down as she looked about to faint. Fortunately I knew from my training that cold,

*clammy skin and fast, shallow breathing is a sign of
shock, so I held her and kept her close. The wound
wasn't as deep as I feared when I looked, but she was
obviously in shock. We cleaned round the cut and
dressed it and she needed some pain relief. I'm glad
we checked it over the following few days because
she'd used an old razor blade and the germs created
an infection and needed antibiotics from the doctor.*

Helen

❓ My son burns himself. What should I do about the injuries?

You can treat a minor burn at home, but if it's larger than a postage
stamp, you'll need professional medical help. If the burn is deep,
then regardless of its size you should seek urgent hospital care.

For minor burns you'll need to run the skin under cool water
immediately to stop any tissue damage. Try to do this within the
first twenty minutes and keep cooling the skin with lukewarm
water for between ten and thirty minutes. Cover the area with
a sterile dressing or cling film or even a clean plastic bag. Don't
apply any creams, ointments, or lotions and don't burst any blisters.
Minor burns fade, although they may take several months, but
deeper burns tend to heal with scars. Children can be particularly
badly affected, developing thick, red, prominent scars as a result of
scalds, but these can fade and be treated with pressure garments,
and silicone can be helpful. Surgery can be used to replace very
severe scars with skin grafts and by putting in extra skin to reduce
tension. You'll need expert medical advice, and don't be afraid to
ask questions and consider all the options and outcomes.

Parent to Parent

*We discovered our son was using a lighter to burn
his skin and it took us ages to believe and accept
that this was something he did, strangely to make*

himself feel better, calmer, and in control again. The marks were on his wrists and his inner arm; he couldn't say why he chose those places but they looked terrible. A number of them were slow to heal and left deep red marks worse than any I'd experienced getting things in and out of the oven, so they must have really hurt him. He didn't seem to want my sympathy and hated it when I got upset, so we just treated the burns in a matter of fact manner without fuss. I pretended not to be affected. I tried to concentrate on the injuries rather than on my feelings, which helped a bit. I saw it as my duty to teach him how to care for the burns and try to stop him from making deeper ones. While I tended the wounds I had an opportunity to talk to him about the self-harming and future burns and injuries. I'm not a nurse and it wasn't something I thought I'd ever be doing for my child but suddenly you're in a situation and you have to deal with it.

Hilary

Check Point

Information about unusual scarring:

- As wounds heal, scar tissue forms, which at first is often red and raised. Over several months, the scar usually becomes flat and pale.

- If there's a lot of tension on a healing wound, the healing area is rather thicker than usual and may continue to thicken for up to six months and appear darker. This is known as a hypertrophic scar.

- Hypertrophic scars are more common in the young and people with darker skin. Some people have an inherited tendency to this type of scarring, and some people naturally make better scars than others.

- The good news is that hypertrophic scars remain contained and can fade over time. They often improve on their own, though it may take a year or more.

- Severe scars can be treated, so encourage your child to see a doctor as soon as possible, who may then recommend you to a plastic surgeon.

? **Our daughter is very embarrassed about the marks she's made on her skin. What can we do to help her disguise them?**

You and your child will probably be very conscious of marks made by self-harm, but try to reassure them that there's a lot that can be done to help them fade. Once a wound is fully healed you can use a number of easily available products. You can find most at your local pharmacy. Some are designed to cool and soothe, such as aloe vera gel and aftersun; others, such as make-up concealers and cosmetic body make-up (available in a range of skin tones), help to disguise marks. Some products have healing properties that ease itching and smooth scars, helping to reduce them. Oils and creams such as Bio-Oil, E45 and cocoa butter moisturize the skin and help keep it smooth and supple. You'll need to watch out for steroid-based products, because they can weaken skin. Silicone plasters, patches, and gels can help any marks fade and flatten. Be reassured that scars do not occur in younger people as often as older people because young skin cells replicate more quickly and fill in the wounded area with normal skin tissue. Remind them that although an injury may look red and angry to begin with, normally it will fade and may even disappear naturally. Having a tattoo to cover scars is sometimes suggested by self-harm organizations, but of course not everyone wants a tattoo, and damaged skin can be weak and not absorb tattooing ink evenly, making it look unsightly.

Parent to Parent

Her doctor said, "Remember how embarrassed you'll be in the summer or when you're wearing your wedding dress," and this seemed to have no effect on her outwardly, but it was something she thought about and something she used to motivate her to reduce the number of times she self-harmed. When her sister got married and wanted her to be a bridesmaid, we had a terrible time persuading her to agree and to wear a short-sleeved dress. It was summer, so my daughter who was to be the bride said that long sleeves would look stupid, even lace ones, so that was not a possibility. My daughter had been using silicone gel, which the doctor had recommended, and this had been really good at helping her scars fade but she was still self-conscious about them, really embarrassed and anxious about people looking at her and staring or even talking about her. We went to the beauty department, as I'd heard that you could get body make-up to match your skin tone. One of my friends had used it to cover up a varicose vein for her holiday, and the make-up had been long lasting and waterproof. We got the right shade and my daughter was really pleased. It saved the day and she used it all the time until her scars faded. They took about a year to fade using the silicone gel, patches, and serum. Naturally we were all worried that they wouldn't fade, but they did.

Lesley

Check Point

Information about hypertrophic and keloid scars:

- According to the British Association of Aesthetic Plastic Surgeons, patients with black skin and patients with fair, freckled skin and red hair tend to produce poor scars, including hypertrophic scars and keloid scars.

- It's not possible to completely prevent hypertrophic scars, so anyone who has previously developed one should inform their doctor or surgeon if they need to have any type of surgery in the future.

- Keloid scars can be confused with hypertrophic scars but are different. Keloids are excessively thick, fibrous, tumour-like growths that extend beyond the wound's original limits.

- Keloid scars can itch, cause pain, and be tender to the touch. Although they're unsightly, they're not dangerous, do not produce any medical complications, and again they can be treated.

? How do we prevent and treat scars?

Some sufferers like to have a reminder of earlier pain and hardship, but most find scarring a real problem to live with (and sometimes therefore a focus for recovery), not only because scarring is unsightly and often hurts but also because of the stares of other people, the potential questions from friends, family, and even strangers, and the resulting self-consciousness.

Scars are a natural part of the healing process when the skin repairs a wound caused by injury. Although no scar can be completely removed, remember that the time skin takes to heal varies according to a number of factors: the degree of damage, the direction of the scar, the nature and quality of the skin, the location of the scar, and how well the wound is cared for. The longer the wound takes to heal, the greater the chance of a noticeable scar, which could take up to a year or more to fade. Normal scars develop during the first forty-eight hours after the wound is closed and can fade within three months.

In a few cases scars can become abnormal, such as hypertrophic and keloid scars, which can occur up to eighteen months later, but these affect only a small percentage of the population. Silicone gel can prevent the formation of abnormal scars. There is also good evidence of its effectiveness in reducing scar-associated pain, itching, and discolouration. The good thing about silicone gel is that it is transparent, odourless, and dries quickly, forming a breathable protection within four to five minutes. Cosmetics and sun block can be used once the gel has dried, which is helpful because fresh injuries or scars are very sensitive to the sun and therefore do require full sun block.

Parent to Parent

I should have taken her back to the doctor for a review and asked to see how the scar was healing, but she was embarrassed and didn't want me to see, so I gave up a bit too easily. Then she complained that it was red and itchy. She had checked on the internet and came downstairs in floods of tears, telling me that her scar had become keloid and she didn't know how it would ever go. She really panicked. I didn't know anything about this, so I made an appointment with a plastic surgeon via my doctor. The surgeon was really nice and very good with her. He didn't ask her any questions about how the scar had formed but explained the facts. It was just bad luck that the scar was an untypical scar, a hypertrophic scar that looked worse than it was. It was not keloid, but he said that even that could be treated. He told her that only about 4 per cent of the population develop a hypertrophic scar but that with silicone gel patches and good pressure the scar would fade, although she'd have to wear a new patch every day and be prepared to give it time, a year maybe. We were obviously very relieved and she did look after the scar well, doing what he said. The patches were expensive and maybe the fright she'd had, as well as the worry that she might develop more unusual scars, did help to focus her mind on recovery.

Rachel

ACTION PLAN

Managing the physical effects of self-harm

- Learn how to treat wounds. There are several organizations that can provide you with information, which are listed in the Useful Contacts section of this book.

- Photocopy the table in the appendix of this book and put it in your first aid kit or near your kitchen or bathroom sink.

- Decide whether you can manage the injury at home. Wounds to the hands, face, joints, and genitals always require the attention of a medical expert. If a wound looks inflamed or infected, then see your doctor or pharmacist.

- If you're in doubt get advice by ringing your doctor or (in the UK) NHS Direct.

- If the wound is serious and if bleeding doesn't stop after ten minutes of pressure, then ring for a paramedic or take your child to an emergency department.

- If your child is conscious, keep the airways open; if not, put them in the recovery position while waiting for an ambulance, and if they're not breathing begin chest compressions.

- Make sure your home medical kit is up to date and includes antiseptic wipes, closure strips, dressings, disposable gloves, and clean plastic bags.

- Apply first aid but also remember to watch out for signs of shock, laying the sufferer down and raising any injured limb.

- If you're not sure whether your child has taken something, be alert to vomiting (sometimes bloodstained), slipping in and out of consciousness, and burning sensations in the throat, chest, and stomach.

- Scars do fade and even abnormal scars can be treated, so do encourage your child to see a doctor quickly. The doctor may recommend you to a board-certified plastic surgeon.

- Picking at scabs and re-opening old injuries is a method of self-harming. Be aware of this and help your child realize that greater scarring can occur as a result.

- Insurance usually doesn't cover cosmetic procedures; however, if scar revision (surgery) is performed to minimize scarring or improve the ability to function, then it may be partially covered. Check your policy or call your carrier/provider to be sure.

- Consider taking a first aid course to give you confidence and the necessary skills to deal with the effects of self-harming.

CHAPTER 11

Finding Professional Medical Help

Your doctor is an important link and a good resource for you, as apart from treating injuries he or she might support you and can refer your child for more specialist treatment. If the injury is severe, the doctor will refer you to your local hospital for medical treatment. If the doctor thinks that your child needs to be assessed for their state of mind and given further psychotherapeutic treatment, then you'll be referred to more specialist services such as the Child and Adolescent Mental Health Services (CAMHS) in the UK. In countries in which there's no state health service you can contact the National Institute for Mental Health where you live or obtain information from your local hospital.

CAMHS are a comprehensive range of services within the UK that provide help and treatment to children and young people with mental health problems. Some of these services are in NHS settings, such as Child and Family Consultation Services, inpatient and outpatient departments of hospitals, or in GP surgeries. Others are based in educational settings, such as schools, colleges and universities, youth centres, and counselling services. Within CAMHS you're able to access psychologists, psychiatrists, family therapists, nursing staff, and other related health experts.

Drug therapy

It's important to remember that children who self-harm often suffer with depression, so their doctor might prescribe antidepressants or you might need to ask. It's usual to have a consultant overseeing this decision if your child is young, and you'll have the opportunity to discuss the benefits and any concerns. If you're worried, please remember that antidepressants can make a huge difference to someone's mood, giving them the ammunition to fight overwhelming sadness and despair. However, it's important to have the right type and dosage, along with the necessary frequent reviews with the doctor and/or consultant.

DID YOU KNOW?
PROFESSIONAL RECOMMENDATIONS

- *The UK NICE (National Institute for Health and Clinical Excellence) guidelines are respected across the world for best practice.*

- *The guidelines for self-harm state that a person's emotional and mental state should be urgently established by a doctor to assess the likely physical risk and that this should be done in an "atmosphere of respect and understanding".*

- *Your child should be treated courteously, with due care and concern.*

- *All people who have self-harmed should be offered a preliminary psychosocial review at the first assessment at the doctor's or on arrival at hospital.*

- *This assessment should determine a person's mental capacity, their willingness to remain for further(psychosocial) assessment, their level of distress (depression, hopelessness, and any risk of suicide), and the possible presence of mental illness.*

- *A doctor should refer them for urgent treatment in the nearest emergency department if there's significant risk and if they've self-poisoned.*

? We feel our daughter's care is unsatisfactory. Is this unusual?

Studies show that many primary care doctors aren't sure how to approach the issues directly with a young person who self-harms or where or how to direct them to the most appropriate services. Doctors have an important role when a young person discloses self-harm, so a doctor's reaction can have a critical influence on their decision to access supportive services. Believing a doctor has a poor understanding of self-harm and lacks experience of helping sufferers may well contribute to the high numbers of young people keeping self-harm from the attention of primary care doctors.

Although there are many doctors who offer great care and understanding, many have little training in self-harm and poor empathy towards patients. In the UK, many GPs admit to not being sure about how to approach this issue with young people. In the United States, an American health foundation found that primary care doctors, who are often the gateway to specialized treatment, are often inadequately trained to identify and diagnose mental health problems.[17] Doctors are sometimes well aware of their limited understanding of self-harming, but they are also concerned about confidentiality and child protection and what they should do for a young person who is waiting to be seen by more specialist services.

Parent to Parent

In retrospect it wasn't the doctor's fault, but we'd been so worried and the wait had been long so our nerves were on edge. I also think we looked to the doctor to have all the answers and therefore our expectations were too high, so the poor man could only disappoint.

It was really hard persuading our daughter to see the doctor and really embarrassing and difficult telling him that our daughter self-harmed, but I thought he'd know what to do and might have shown some sympathy. He just looked shocked and surprised, which made me feel very alone. He wasn't interested in why she self-harmed and didn't ask her about her feelings – just asked me if she was a nice teenager, as if only nasty teenagers self-harmed. Next he took the stance that this was a pretty common occurrence nowadays – that most teenagers self-harm, as if it were catching and that nobody could do anything about it. He offered no suggestions for how we should try to manage the self-harming, let alone help her overcome it. He wasn't interested in discussing her anxiety or even referring her to consultants for them to assess her for medication. Most surprisingly, he didn't even ask to see the marks she'd made by the cutting. All he did was to give me a link to some websites and photocopy something for her about anger management. She didn't have anger problems. I left feeling very unsupported, and my daughter, who already felt guilty, left feeling ashamed and even more of a burden.

Melanie

FACT OR FICTION?
. . . .

Self-harming is not often serious enough to warrant medical care.

No! Self-harm is one of the top five causes of acute medical admission in the UK. However, most individuals who self-harm and present to hospital do so after a self-poisoning episode.[18]

On average there will be around ten to fifteen children and adolescents who self-harm within a GP practice in the UK. Most young people who do visit their doctor for self-harming go with physical symptoms, such as burns or cuts, not always attributed to the harming.

? **What medical treatment is available for self-harm?**

Anyone who has self-harmed should be offered treatment for the physical consequences, regardless of their willingness to accept psychosocial assessment or psychiatric treatment. If your child has self-harmed and has presented before, each subsequent episode of self-harming should be treated in its own right, because the reasons for the harming may be different. There have been many complaints by sufferers that pain relief has been withheld or has been inadequate if suturing or other painful treatment is needed; therefore, you may be able to oversee this and help your child receive the appropriate recommended care.

Your child should be given full information about the treatment options and the opportunity to give meaningful and informed consent before any procedure (for example, taking them to hospital by ambulance) or before any treatment is begun. If your child is already seeing a therapist, then together they may have developed a written care plan or a "Crisis Card", which tells medical staff how your child would like to be treated.

Fewer than half of those who present to UK emergency departments for self-harming are actually then admitted to a ward.[19] NICE guidelines recommend that a child is offered an overnight stay in a paediatric ward while waiting for assessment, and you may be relieved that your child is kept safe this way. If this is the first time they've been to hospital, you'll probably be very concerned and not sure what might happen. Depending on your child's age, circumstances, and mental health, they may be offered admission to an adolescent psychiatric unit. Prior to any decisions being made, you should expect the admitting team to have talked to you and gained your consent for a mental health assessment. A paediatrician should normally have overall responsibility for the treatment and care of children and young people admitted following an act of self-harm. It's usual to have a consultation with the CAMHS team, who will include you and your family as well as your child, sometimes bringing in education staff and social services.

Parent to Parent

The nurse could see that we were extremely anxious, highly stressed, and tired. We'd been seeing our doctor and had been to the emergency department once before, so we wondered if they'd think, "Here we go again." We hadn't seen this nurse before, and she was very kind and all smiles considering it was half past one in the morning. She first tried to calm and get a relationship with our daughter and then saw to the injury. She also did the relevant general observations like temperature, pulse, and blood pressure and asked us whether she was allergic to any medication or substance, such as latex, as she'd be applying adhesive self-closure strips and maybe even surgical glue. She was also vigilant about shock and invited our daughter to lie down, because we thought she might faint. The nurse asked her to chat with a doctor once she felt a little calmer and was patched up. By that time she felt able to answer the questions he had for her. They were all very nice, even though they knew she'd been there before, and it helped us feel less tense and apologetic.

Roger

Check Point

Information about accident and emergency departments:

- Although 62 per cent of adolescents in a New Zealand study reported a positive experience,[20] some patients in the UK felt they were treated differently from others in accident and emergency, attributing this to the self-harming.

- Many patients who self-harm complained that staff concentrated entirely on their physical needs and ignored their emotional health.

- Sufferers record lack of kindness, no anaesthesia given for suturing, and being kept waiting for unacceptable lengths of time.

- Positive experiences were associated with being updated and provided with regular check-ups while waiting.

? We want to be present and included in her care. Is this allowed?

If you're accompanying your child to hospital or joining them there, then you may want to be with them during their assessment and treatment. Remember that if they're sixteen or over, they have the right to decide whether or not to accept treatment and they can ask to be seen alone. Your child is allowed to request a family member, friend, or advocate to accompany them; however, the interview forming the initial assessment is done in private so they can discuss any issues relating to their relationship with you, their carer. You should expect healthcare professionals to provide you with emotional support and understand your distress and anxiety. As parents carry so much emotion and unnecessary guilt, you may feel that staff suspect or blame you, which can make the experience extremely difficult for all. Although it's hard, try not to allow your fears and anxieties to spill over into anger and frustration towards staff. It's not unusual for dads in particular to find this hard, thereby inviting unnecessary attention.

Parent to Parent

Thankfully, I was warned to keep my emotions under control. I found it hard not to blame my son for all the grief he was causing us. I was exasperated by it all and nobody wants to be sitting in the accident and emergency department of an evening, so all our emotions were running high. I think the medics sympathized a little, although their first job was to clean and suture the deep cut on my son's leg. My having a go at him and my son arguing with me didn't help. The doctor asked me to wait outside and I felt a bit humiliated, which got me wondering whether the doctor thought I was responsible. My wife was crying and a nurse was looking after her. After a while we were both asked to go into a separate waiting room to talk to another doctor and probably to give us some private space. No one accused us of anything; we just felt bad about it.

Tim

Check Point

Facts about medical admissions:

- The summer months, particularly May and July, when school and college exams are taken, see the highest number of hospital admissions for self-harming.[21]

- During the same time period, December had the lowest recorded figure overall.

- Children and adolescents under sixteen years of age account for about 5 per cent of all self-harm episodes presenting to hospital in the UK.

- Some 10-15 per cent of these cases are those who present often and have a history of self-harm.[22]

❓ Our daughter has taken an overdose. How will she be treated in hospital?

If your child is under sixteen and is being treated under the NHS in the UK, they'll need to be seen by appropriately trained children's doctors and nurses, because they have a number of special needs, given their vulnerability. Staff should be adequately trained to assess the mental capacity of different ages and have access to specialist staff members. Assessments should be the same for adults who self-harm, but you and your family will probably be invited in to the assessment. It's recommended that the assessment and treatment should take place in a separate children's area of the emergency department. Activated charcoal is often used to flush out aspirin, but those who need treatment for paracetamol overdose will need a drip and a three or four day stay in hospital. It's usual for your family doctor to be notified by the hospital so that he or she can offer aftercare.

Parent to Parent

We were obviously very concerned and really surprised to be kept waiting for hours. Nobody came to reassure us or seemed interested in examining our daughter. She'd taken an overdose but was allowed to sit there. Eventually the nurse ushered us into a cubicle and, without any pleasantries, told us to take away all medications and other means of self-harm from our home, as this advice was part of their recommendations. We assumed she was just going through the procedure in a rather inhuman way and thought we were stupid, as we'd already done that long ago but unfortunately our daughter had bought the tablets herself. We were also told to wait outside while her colleagues interviewed our daughter. They merely asked her what she'd taken and how many, and then she was told to wait in the corridor with us. Thankfully they didn't consider it a serious attempt, but we were there for over five hours and I found it hard to keep calm. We never saw anyone after that, except to be told that we could go home. Our daughter had no discussion or interest shown about her emotional state, we didn't see anyone trained in child and adolescent mental health, and there was no follow-up with her family doctor. We were all really shocked and I was very angry.

Phil

ACTION PLAN

Finding professional medical help

- Encourage your child and reassure them about seeing a doctor.

- Consider which doctor in your practice would be most appropriate and sympathetic.

- Stay in touch with your family doctor, even if your child is receiving more specialist care, so he or she can monitor the situation and give you some support, perhaps signposting you to a counsellor or support group.

- If you're accompanying your child to hospital, keep them calm and supported.

- Try to keep communication open between you and your child's consultant, nurse, and the rest of the team involved in their treatment.

- If you feel you haven't been included or that you don't understand the options or approach they're taking, then ask your professionals for more information.

- If your child needs stitches, make sure they receive adequate anaesthesia and/or analgesia.

- If your child is unsure about accepting treatment, particularly if they're an adult, help them gain as much information about it as possible and know where it's located.

- If your child is referred to a specialized unit, look it up together on the internet or see if you can visit beforehand, maybe even meeting one or two key members of staff.

- Children aged fifteen have certain rights relating to confidentiality and consent to treatment, and those over sixteen have full rights.

- Talk with your child about the future benefits of accepting treatment, and put some incentives in place.

- If they are adults admitted to a ward, help them with practical matters, such as visits and managing their affairs back home. If they're younger, help them to carry on with school or college work. Worry about things like this might be an obstacle to their accepting treatment.

- Help them stay occupied while they are in hospital, providing artwork or crafts, games, magazines, and hobbies.

- Help them feel loved, supported, encouraged, and not forgotten. Arrange visits from friends and bring cards and letters, photographs, their own duvet cover, and other reminders of home.

- Make sure an aftercare plan is in place before your child is discharged from hospital or a specialized unit.

CHAPTER 12

Finding and Receiving Therapy

Even if you're managing at home without the need for professional medical help, you may feel that your child would benefit from some form of therapy. A course of psychotherapy sessions provides not only support but also a method of working that often focuses on addressing the issues causing the self-harming, and helps the sufferer to rethink and re-evaluate their emotional responses and behaviour. Therapy usually seeks to address the factors associated with self-harm, including depression, anxiety, impulsivity, feelings of hopelessness, and difficulty with problem solving.

Your doctor may refer your child for therapeutic treatment via the CAMHS or adult mental health services, particularly if their mental health is causing concern or the harm is severe. Your views about how you and your family are coping should also be taken into account. If you feel you don't have the resources to support your child or the harming seems out of control, then you should talk to your doctor for advice. Of course you can also access therapeutic help privately, and there are many trained counsellors who have expertise with self-harm. ABC has a database of counsellors trained to support clients who self-harm, and there are counselling organizations under Useful Contacts at the back of this book. If your child has self-harmed several times and been taken to the accident and emergency department often, they may be offered developmental group psychotherapy with other young people who have repeatedly self-harmed. This should include at least six sessions and further group therapy may also be offered.

Which therapy?

There are many forms of therapy available. Therapeutic treatment includes a number of talking therapies – psychotherapies based on a variety of approaches, such as cognitive behavioural therapy, dialectical behaviour therapy, problem-solving therapy, person-centred therapy, and hypnotherapy. The focus for self-harming tends to be on developing problem-solving and coping skills as an alternative to self-harm. There's been little research so far to see which treatments work best for young people, but developmental group therapy and multi-systemic therapy (MST) are both known to reduce rates of self-harm among children and adolescents.[23] In addition, there are arts-based therapies and family therapies that harness the support and increase the understanding of family members.

DID YOU KNOW?
FACTS ABOUT GROUP THERAPY

- *Group therapy programmes for adolescents who repeatedly self-harmed were found more effective than conventional care, such as non-specific counselling and family sessions, for reducing future instances of self-harm.*

- *Group therapy involves both problem-solving and cognitive behavioural therapy and is based on themes that are known to be associated with self-harm, such as hopelessness, problems with family and school relationships, depression, guilt, and anger.*

- *Group therapy also improves school attendance but does not affect depression, which is a key factor in self-harm among children and adolescents.[24]*

? Our doctor has recommended cognitive behavioural therapy. What is this and what does it do?

Cognitive behavioural therapy (CBT) is a well-used method that addresses current problems and behaviour, looking at ways to rethink responses. It can be a very effective treatment for depression, anxiety, and a variety of problems and conditions, notably Obsessive Compulsive Disorder (OCD) and eating disorders, and is often used for young people and adolescents. The UK's Royal College of Psychiatrists describes CBT as "a way of talking about how you think about yourself, the world and other people and how what you do affects your thoughts and feelings. CBT can help you to change how you think ('Cognitive') and what you do ('Behaviour')." It focuses on the "here and now" problems and difficulties, unlike some of the other talking treatments that focus on the causes of distress or symptoms in the past.

The main aim of CBT is to change behaviour, which is done by applying techniques with a focus on problem solving, including skills training, homework, diary cards, and behavioural analysis. Many people benefit from this type of approach, particularly if they're good at seeing connections and are prepared to work on recovery. CBT is a one-to-one structured course lasting several months. There are online CBT programmes as well as telephone counselling for those who don't wish to sit face to face with someone or for whom travelling is a problem.

Parent to Parent

We didn't know anything about therapy and hadn't experienced it before so CBT was new to us, but we were told that it was effective and often used. The therapy didn't look way back to the past but centred more on her current thinking. We picked up some tips that we could use at home when she was thinking badly about herself and voicing her criticisms. Our daughter learned that the way she regarded herself, the thoughts she had about herself, without forgetting the things in her past, were the reasons why she felt the need to cut herself. It took a long time for her to begin to even think things through, let alone confide in anyone. Her therapist helped her to see the cycle she was trapped in while also giving her respect, understanding and continual patience, even during episodes of continued self-harm. We were surprised that her harming became worse once the therapy was underway, and this frightened us, but her therapist reassured us. She helped our daughter without judgment to see that she was in effect punishing herself, but trying to cut out memories and pain, re-stamping herself with her own marks. This allowed the caring side of her to tend to her injuries and to heal herself. She said she was learning to be a survivor rather than a victim. This made some sense to me.

She had to write her thoughts down in a diary in response to the questions and headings, and after a while could see certain patterns of behaviour and begin to identify certain thoughts and feelings that triggered a harming episode. Although to begin with the self-harming intensified, partly because she had to think about it so much, the slow work of support and belief started to result in changes to her attitudes about herself. Eventually some of her self-harming behaviour began to change, but it was slow, very slow indeed, so that a lot of people gave up on her, even some of our own family, which was very upsetting. Although I didn't often see her counsellor, knowing that she was working with our daughter and helping her made a big difference to how I felt.

Megan

FACT OR FICTION?

The aim of family therapy is to find problems within the family.

No! Family therapy is not aimed at finding fault with the family. Neither does it exist to provide therapy for parents and siblings, although often that's desperately needed. Its primary aim is to get everyone working together to help the child who self-harms and for the family to be happy and united again. Of course, family therapy is therefore useful for a range of other issues besides self-harming, such as bereavement, coming to terms with cancer, anxiety disorders, agoraphobia, eating disorders, and autism spectrum disorders.

? Our daughter won't continue the sessions. Is this common and what can we do?

The main problems associated with any therapy are when the client doesn't really want to be there, or when the therapeutic relationship doesn't work. The relationship between therapist and client is crucial, and when it works well your child will find the therapist a real source of steadfast support and guidance. Young people can come to realize that their therapist is someone "outside" the family who is there just for them, more objective, and, unlike parents, won't get upset and take anything personally. However, in order to establish that relationship you need to encourage them to continue.

Children are particularly hard to engage in counselling because they often feel pressured into going. If your child feels coerced or threatened, then regardless of how good a therapist they have or how strong their relationship with the therapist might become, the therapy isn't going to match expectations or even continue. It is very difficult for therapists to counsel clients who refuse to open up and who miss appointments or blame the therapist for being substandard. Professionals providing therapy to adolescents, either individually or as a family, should be sensitive to any tensions that may undermine success. Many therapists are happy to work with you as parents, in addition to working confidentially with your child, and be part of a multidisciplinary team.

If your child continues to refuse to go, try finding the deeper cause of the refusal, reassure them about going, and try to come to an agreement – a compromise that they should try for at least three more sessions. If that doesn't work, consider asking the therapist to provide telephone counselling or, if necessary, find another therapist.

Parent to Parent

I'd put all my hopes in her seeing a counsellor, and I'd had quite a search to find who I thought was the right one, so when she said she wasn't going again, I was really disappointed and felt hopeless. When calm I asked her why and she explained she didn't like her, didn't think she was any good or would help her. I knew enough not to argue with her and try to force her, but I did say that I recognized that she might have some doubts but that it wasn't fair to judge the counsellor on one session; that she should try another couple of sessions to get to know her better. She said she'd think about it and we left it at that. However, I thought that her older sister might be good for her to talk to because she admires her and listens to her, so I got her to call her to talk about it. It worked because when the next appointment came round, my younger daughter was ready to go without a word from me. I think if I'd insisted she went or pleaded with her then she would've refused and then wouldn't have been able to back down. She did carry on the sessions over the months and really rated her counsellor. I think the first session must be difficult for a lot of people and that those supporting them have to understand this and be quite clever when it comes to encouraging them to go and keep on going.

Gill

Check Point

Information about therapy:

- Therapy means a commitment of several months and is hard work, as many people find that it brings painful issues or memories to the surface.

- Initially self-harming can become worse, so both you and your child should be prepared.

- Remember that the journey back from seeing the therapist can be a turbulent time. Your tactful enquiries might be met with hostility, or your child might be sullen and silent.

- If you're engaging a private therapist, try to find one who works within a thirty-minute journey from your home.

? **I've heard that dialectical behaviour therapy is a recommended therapy for self-harm. What is it and how can it help?**

Dialectical behaviour therapy (DBT) was developed as a response to those who dropped out of CBT therapy because they felt that the strong emphasis on change ignored their past suffering and underestimated their feelings of loss of control. This doesn't mean that the CBT techniques were ineffective, but that emotionally sensitive clients found the techniques difficult and distressing when applied on their own. Consequently, DBT is the only therapy known to be effective in reducing self-harm among certain adult populations, particularly those with borderline personality disorder.

DBT adds "acceptance strategies" into the treatment, with the aim of balancing acceptance with change to therefore meet the needs of those who have found CBT difficult and invalidating. Using acceptance strategies, DBT therapists can show clients that although their harmful behaviour isn't in their best interest in the long term, it makes sense, as it's often the only way they've learned to deal with intense emotions. It accepts that, previously, such behaviour might have led to positive consequences in the short term. The therapist can enable their client to balance acceptance with change, and over time challenge and replace their behaviours by learning more effective ways of coping with their emotions.

Parent to Parent

For my daughter self-harm is about anger, uncontrollable feelings, and frustration because of what's happened to her. She doesn't know exactly what she's feeling and how to handle that confusion. It all builds up. She's discovered that extreme anger really accelerates the need and finds calming herself extremely difficult. I think that if you keep it a secret, the difficulties of being alone with your feelings fuel the cycle of self-harm. So talking to someone you trust and who doesn't judge you, like a counsellor, is really helpful. She found counselling helped her to understand her feelings of low self-esteem and herself a bit better. She's also learned to accept not understanding how she's feeling and be content with that, realizing that she can't explain everything. Learning to accept that has been quite a journey. For perfectionists and people who like to be always in control of their thinking, it's hard. She found DBT a great approach because it gave her a solid relationship with her counsellor and her group, with more contact time than her previous therapy. DBT lets her phone her therapist if she's in melt-down, as part of crisis coaching, but she's not allowed to call straight away after self-harming, and I think this gives her more of a focus to try to stop. My daughter found the skills training hard work but helpful, and she got a lot from the diaries she had to keep. She's gradually learning a different response to her past hurts and her present uncontrollable reactions. She can begin to see a future now.

Lauren

? We've been offered family therapy. What can we expect?

The UK Association of Family Therapy describes it as supporting change with individuals and also in their relationships in the family and beyond, so that children, young people, and/or those important to them are supported in continued recovery.

The idea of family therapy can be daunting for parents, as, understandably, you can imagine that the therapist is looking to find fault with you or your parenting skills or perhaps even blame you for your child's self-harming. Perhaps you fear that something you've said or done, or not said or not done, will be brought up. Do remember that the sessions are not designed to blame you or attack you. The aim is to get everyone talking and looking together at ways in which you can help your child, and for your child to be able to accept that help and to make progress towards recovery. The therapist will recognize the suffering caused to all family members by the self-harming and will help all come to terms with the behaviour, resolve conflicts, and identify issues to help the child who self-harms recover.

Parent to Parent

I was extremely nervous and really on my guard. I overanalysed everything the counsellor said and asked me, and I was on the defensive. The first session was pretty tense. My son sat there silent and sullen, his brother glaring at him, and our younger daughter sat on the floor drawing in her colouring book and ignoring everything else. My husband didn't want to be there, and I could sense smouldering anger and resentment in him. He felt that therapy would be a waste of time and was angry about having to take time off work. I was so wrung out with fear and lack of sleep that I'm sure I must have appeared very hyper. The therapist was really nice and relaxed, and immediately we could tell she understood all the typical reactions – a lot of our heartache too. She was completely unfazed by our son's silent rudeness and handled the whole session confidently but calmly. She gave me hope that we could all get through. The first session was a "getting to know you session", and although our son still refused to speak, he did say yes to going back for the next session, so we decided not to say anything more on the way home and wait for him to speak about it if he chose to, even though I was aching to hear something positive from him.

Karen

Check Point

The four skills of DBT based on cognitive behaviour:

- "Core Mindfulness" enables someone to become more clearly aware of the contents of their experience and to develop the ability to stay with that experience in the present moment.

- "Emotional Regulation" focuses on learning to identify, regulate, and change distressing emotions.

- "Distress Tolerance" teaches someone to accept and tolerate emotional states if they can't be immediately changed.

> • "Interpersonal Effectiveness" focuses on effective ways of achieving one's objectives with other people – for example, to ask for what one wants, to say no and have it taken seriously, to maintain relationships, and to maintain self-esteem in interactions with other people.[25]

❓ How helpful are support groups?

Support groups for your child and self-help groups for you as a carer do exist in certain counties in the UK. Parents and sufferers can find this kind of group support really useful. This type of support group might be more suitable for adults and much older children, but it depends on whether your child feels that they would benefit from talking about their feelings in front of others and listening to the stories, thoughts, and feelings of other group members and their underlying issues – and perhaps being influenced by them all.

There's been little research conducted into self-help groups in the UK. The organization of self-help groups is more advanced in the USA and more recognized by medical professionals as being valuable in extending the health and mental health care system, according to the Self-Help Network.[26] Studies of people who'd experienced acute long-term mental ill health found that those who attended a network of self-help groups needed fewer medical services.[27] The idea behind self-help is one of equality and empowerment. If your child attends a group, they'll be regarded as an equal among the members, with everyone having a valuable contribution, and this can help to increase self-esteem. Self-help groups are run by the members and have no input from professionals, which can be positive for some, especially those who have had difficult experiences with health care.

The groups provide a safe environment through acceptance, so that those struggling with self-harm can look at their coping mechanisms and what lies behind them. Groups can offer an opportunity for sufferers to better understand their self-harm by sharing common experiences and knowledge, by being helped by others and by helping others in turn.

Parent to Parent

Our daughter joined a self-help group, and to be honest I thought she'd just take on other people's worries and life histories and that maybe by talking about the harming she'd do it more. I'm quite a private person and sitting round in a group talking about hurting and inner feelings would be something I'd hate, but there wasn't much help around that she could afford so the group was all that was available. It turned out to be very beneficial and a great source of strength and support. She said it gave her hope, as there were people there who were further along in their recovery. She's had some damage done in the past by people who couldn't accept her, so having an understanding environment – a place where nobody judged anybody – was really helpful to her. She said her friends there gave her the strength to recover and support when she had setbacks. She felt less lonely and isolated and we saw that this had a real effect on her confidence and her self-esteem. It might not be for everyone, but for my daughter the group was really helpful and she made some lasting friends and mentors.

Paul

ACTION PLAN

Finding and receiving therapy

- If your child is offered therapy, encourage them to think well of the process.

- Encourage them to keep going to sessions.

- Find the right therapeutic treatment to suit your child.

- Remember that therapy sessions are hard work for your child, so allow them to tell you what they want, when they want.

- Remember to ask your child if they mind people knowing they're undergoing therapy or want someone to be informed.

- If you're seeking a private therapist, make sure they're fully qualified and accredited and that they have experience of counselling those who self-harm.

- Don't put all your hope for recovery into your therapist or in a particular therapeutic approach.

- Where possible choose a therapist near your child's home, as long journeys are another pressure and may provide an excuse not to go.

- If you're invited to any sessions, particularly family therapy, then make every effort to develop a good relationship with the therapist.

- Remember to hold back and allow your child to speak and develop a rapport with their therapist.

- Family therapy can appear threatening, so try not to think you're being blamed or that your actions, relationships, and parenting skills are under attack.

- Try to encourage reluctant members of the immediate family to attend therapy sessions, but don't force them to go to every one.

- Try to encourage those taking part in family therapy to keep calm and not to direct any anger at the therapist or your child.

- Be aware that many therapists work as part of a disciplinary team with other professionals working to support your child, such as your doctor, community psychiatric nurses, and psychologists.

CHAPTER 13

Overcoming Self-Harm

There isn't a single definition of recovery in mental health, but according to the UK's leading mental health research charity, The Mental Health Foundation, the guiding principle is hope. It's important that you believe in recovery for your child and that you convey this belief to them – in fact, that you keep this hope alive for them while they are too fragile or depressed to own it themselves. Part of the problem for those struggling with self-harm is not being able to understand what recovery really is or to accept that it is achievable. At ABC we can maintain the hope of recovery with confidence, not just because of my own experience and the experience of the many parents ABC has supported whose children have gone on to recover from self-harm, but also because of the many recovered sufferers themselves we have supported. A number of these sufferers were adults, and their parents therefore played a supportive role rather than a driving one.

Recovery is a journey

The Foundation also makes the point that recovery is not about getting rid of problems but about helping people to "look beyond mere survival and existence. It encourages them to move forward, set new goals, and do things and develop relationships that give their lives meaning. It is about seeing beyond a person's mental health problems, recognizing and fostering their abilities, interests, and dreams. The process is a journey that requires optimism and commitment from everyone and requires a well-organized system of support from parents, family, friends, and professionals."[28]

DID YOU KNOW?
FACTS ABOUT RECOVERY

- *Putting recovery into action means "focusing care on supporting recovery and building the resilience" of those struggling with self-harming," not just on treating or managing their symptoms," according to The Mental Health Foundation.*

- *Those who self-harm may need medical care from time to time or more regularly if their harming is frequent or severe. They may also need psychotherapeutic help or even some intensive outpatient support from the community psychiatric team in order to help them recover.*

- *Serious self-harming (particularly if it's part of a wider mental health illness) may require even more intensive inpatient treatment.*

- *Good treatment addresses the underlying causes and concerns of the patient and supports them personally as they learn new and less damaging behaviours. Learning these is vital to recovery.*

How should we view recovery?

Try to remember that the recovery process focuses on the person and not just their behaviour or condition. Recovery can happen in fits and starts, sometimes with many setbacks, but these don't necessarily take someone right back to the beginning. Please remember that recovery from self-harm is achievable. Naturally, you'll have times, as I did, when you wonder whether self-harm will ever move into the past and your child *will* learn to recover, or whether the progress you're seeing really is heralding *long-standing* recovery, but do try to share these understandable worries and heartache with the people supporting you and not with your child.

Parent to Parent

I like the term "overcoming" rather than "recovery", because so many people associate recovery with being back to normal, as one would be after a physical illness, and because the word "recovery" seems to imply speed and ease, neither of which is applicable to overcoming self-harm. I much prefer the word "overcoming" because it expresses the terrible struggle and the great efforts of my daughter and others like her. It also conveys the emotions and hard work of us, her family, supporting her daily over the years, and it took quite a few years for the self-harming to fade into the past. I've come to realize that it's not all about her ceasing to self-harm, although of course I'm so pleased she doesn't need it any more. It's more about her stability, how she's learned to understand herself and grow confident and secure. Overcoming self-harm grew alongside her own personal growth: she learned to take risks, particularly with relationships, and cope with criticism, hurt, and rejection, without taking it out on herself, and on her body. It's about her courage to take risks, and, with regard to the harming behaviour, her effort and persistence first to delay it, and then to replace it. Of course there were times when she slipped back, but she carried on and tried again. She says she feels she doesn't need it any more and that's a real joy to hear.

Jane

FACT OR FICTION?

Once you self-harm you're always a self-harmer.

No! This is one of the most damaging, blinkered, and misinformed views. Recovery is achievable, and with support, strategies, and time, the urge to self-harm

> *can be replaced. According to young people, the most common methods for resisting the urge to self-harm were keeping busy, being around friends, talking to someone about how you feel and writing about how you feel, doing sports or exercise recreationally, and removing the means/instruments typically used to self-harm from home.*[29]

? Are there any factors that particularly help recovery from self-harm?

Parents often ask this fundamental question. Although there's still little research about the process of recognizing and adapting to alternative coping strategies, a study based on adults who had stopped self-harming found that three important factors for recovery stood out: having a strong, steadfast, supportive friend, relative or professional; having a good reason or motivation for overcoming self-harming; and the feeling and desire to take or regain control.

As parents we should remember that young people experiencing self-harm said that being believed in, listened to, and understood were important aspects of support generally and also in recovery. They also valued having help to make sense of their experiences and solve problems. It's crucial that you or anyone else supporting your child during the recovery process encourages them to develop their skills and supports them to achieve their goals.

Parent to Parent

Our daughter told us that for her there was a combination of thoughts and desires which motivated her towards recovery. Firstly she wanted to be normal, to be with her friends without issues. Embarrassment was a factor – going to college meant she didn't want scars. But it wasn't as easy as just thinking about it differently and merely stopping – of course not. Other factors were at play too. Previously because she was so sensitive she'd found it hard to handle horrible comments from other people and lots of work stress without using self-harm. However, she gradually learned to phone (or go and see) her friend, someone she considered totally trustworthy with whom she could talk and let out her emotions. She saw that friend as someone who was her anchor, who helped her to look again at the criticisms of others and to rethink it all, looking at it from different viewpoints.

She found goals, rewards, and motivation were important but that it wasn't a clear, easy, instant formula. It was about taking steps and making certain decisions; also having better feelings towards stopping the harming. Once the need wasn't so great, she felt it was easier to refrain. She said she didn't feel the need to self-harm any more because she felt she'd become a different person. She was also on a good amount of medication and only having relapses into self-harm when her medication had run out or the dosage wasn't strong enough, so that was significant.

It was good to see that she'd learned better coping strategies generally in life – some were about keeping busy, definitely better problem solving, and better resources to calm herself and cope. Her friend was there for her throughout it all – the worst times with mood disturbance and bad attacks of self-harm with accident and emergency, doctors, counselling, and all that – so there was a part of her that wanted to show her friend that she could overcome it. She also wanted to do it for herself. She'd had a serious scare with her last overdose attempt and that was another reason for wanting to overcome the self-harming. Her friend put no pressure on her, she just believed in her. We all did. Gradually stopping self-harm increased her own self-belief, made her feel strong and improved her confidence. She was proud of herself for the changes she'd made and so were we.

Emily

Check Point

Some views of recovery by those who have recovered:

- Recovered sufferers recognize the benefits of increased freedom – from shame, guilt, and obsessive thoughts.

- They discover a newfound confidence, a wider perspective, and new opportunities.

- They find that recovery means not being afraid of being different and that their self-esteem, self-acceptance, and dignity have greatly improved.

- Letting go and finding a new identity is also a feature of recovery for many.

- Learning to cope in new and different ways without fear of losing control is important.

- Many recovered sufferers find that an important aspect of recovery is allowing themselves to make mistakes and not taking things out on themselves when things go wrong.

? What part can we play in recovery?

You've probably realized by now that all the previous chapters are actually about recovery, from helping you to better understand self-harm and its causes both in a general sense and specifically as it relates to your child, to providing suggestions for coping and preparing for recovery. All of this is meant to guide you as you help your child to overcome self-harm.

So whether your child is young and living at home or an adult, please remember there's a lot you can do – even if it's subtle – and there are things to beware of. You should remember that you can't push your child into recovery, setting it at *your* pace, and you can't bribe or blackmail them to stop harming. "No harm contracts" have been found not to work, so it really isn't helpful to make your child agree a contract between you or between them and their counsellor promising not to self-harm. Ignoring self-harm, being angry about it, and buying into the myths and stereotypical thinking won't help your child either. They need good, active, practical, and supportive help. The good news is that you *can* help them and that often they want your help, even though they may appear not to.

Many clinicians agree that the role of parents is vital in giving steadfast support, love, and respect. How much you can guide will depend on the age of your child, your relationship with them, and how entrenched their self-harming has become. They need to know that with help, they can overcome self-harm. You may be able to help them to discover the triggers, supporting them as they learn to rethink their responses. You can help them to learn different or better ways of communication, to release emotions, and to solve problems. You can encourage them to discover and adhere to new strategies for minimizing harm and delaying harming so that gradually their self-harming reduces in frequency and severity. You may be able to guide them towards seeking professional help, helping them to undertake treatment – to stick with therapy even if they are tempted to pull out. Your support will involve encouragement and continual belief in them, as well as practical acts of caring, such as driving them to appointments and nursing them when necessary.

Parent to Parent

We kept reassuring her and trying to help her to view her problems in a more rational way – not to over-analyse everything or see herself as totally responsible for what people thought or said. Relationship difficulties caused her the most problems, and helping her find solutions required a lot of talking and patience. She learned to accept criticism as merely someone's personal opinion, which could have been wrong, or that they were just tired or grumpy. She learned a different and wider perspective. When she became angry and beside herself with frustration we helped her to" hold the thoughts" by holding her, then talking to her and comforting her so she wouldn't have to act immediately in a harmful way to release the feelings. We suggested she try different ways to calm herself. She began to understand that crying was OK, without feeling it was bad or shameful or that it should be replaced with self-harm. She learned that when she was in this state it was better to go to sleep.

It did exhaust us but we love her and wanted to help because it's so upsetting to see your child that distressed so often. It's good to know that she thought we'd helped her discover better ways of coping and solving her problems.

Jane

Check Point

Further views on recovery by those who have recovered:

- Recovered sufferers find that they can accept themselves and see themselves as they really are.

- They feel they can let go of the past and look to the future and move on.

- Accepting change and the things that can't be changed is a feature of recovery.

- Recovery brings peace of mind. They no longer feel as anxious, trapped, or static.

- The ability to care for oneself and being able to give enough to oneself and others is experienced by recovered sufferers.

- Instead of feeling unworthy, an improved self-esteem helps them feel deserving of recovery.

? **Is there anything that we should or shouldn't do?**

Supporting someone who's in the early stages of recovery often involves hearing them battling their conflicting feelings and taking a very negative view of their own recovery, expressing bleakness and despair. If you're prepared for this you can keep your child encouraged and motivated – to believe in their ability to eventually overcome self-harming. Your child may not be able to make progress without professional help, and it's probably down to you (especially if your child still lives at home) to find that help, and support them as they accept it.

It's wise to remember that the supportive role also becomes a very protective one during the years of your child's self-harming, and that understandable protectiveness can remain while they're attempting recovery. Therefore, if we're not careful, our children can feel smothered and find it hard to learn to break their dependency on us. It can be very hard to know when to let go a little and when to step in for them, but hopefully you'll find that you need to step in less as your child is encouraged to make progress.

Parent to Parent

My daughter's psychotherapist encouraged me to go along with her pace of recovery rather than to dictate it by my own enthusiasm and desire for her to get better. Allowing her space to vent her feelings was hard because I imagined that any difficult time would cause her to relapse into self-harming again. I had to keep myself busy and my mind occupied otherwise I would have chased after her all the time or listened outside her bedroom door. I had to trust that with our support and the help of the therapist she would continue to progress. When things did go wrong and her emotions ran high, understanding her and loving her through the rages was very important to her recovery. So too was keeping her focused and occupied.

Looking back, some of her first steps towards recovery included the lessening of the outbursts (first in size and then in frequency) and regaining a sense of humour, which had been lost during the worst times. She didn't like being praised for harming less because she said that made her think about it all the more and she didn't like the fuss and attention. So we had to learn to comment on or praise her for other achievements instead.

I tried not to question her all the time about how she was managing either, although I was longing to hear about school, work, and friendships, but I did realize that I couldn't always quiz her and that it was often better if she started the conversation. She was having therapy so was very aware of anything I said that sounded like a counsellor. We did have some heart to hearts when it seemed appropriate. Needless to say, we got it wrong sometimes and the recovery period was not without some door slamming and shouting.

Jane

ACTION PLAN

Overcoming self-harm

- Hold on to the belief that recovery is possible.

- Remember that ups and downs and setbacks are part of recovery.

- Don't lose hope yourself or blame your child during setbacks.

- Be careful not to put pressure on them to stop self-harming.

- Make sure your child knows that they must choose the pace of recovery.

- Make sure that your child is enabled to choose recovery for their own benefit, not to please others.

- Don't use emotional blackmail to bring about recovery.

- Help re-focus them and motivate them while being sensitive to their mood.

- Encourage the rest of your family to be sensitive and not quiz them about self-harming.

- If you're unsure of how to help them as they recover, ask them.

- Let them try different healthy techniques to delay and reduce harming.

- Give them space to see themselves as someone trying out recovery.

- Make time for them and allow them to discuss problems with you.

- Remind them of how they've resolved conflicts or coped well, to show them they can repeat healthier coping strategies.

- Discuss "mistakes" calmly and help them look at reasons.

- Talk with them about cause and effect, and help them consider the consequences of any action, not just the self-harming.

- Be wise and alert when situations threaten recovery, giving them extra support.

CHAPTER 14

Living Life Free from Self-Harm

For any addictive behaviour that's overcome and with old coping strategies replaced with new ones, there will be situations and pressures that challenge recovery, risking relapse. Although we know that some relapse is part of recovery, relapse is really disappointing for parents and loved ones, for surrounding it lies the panic of being back to square one, with recovery totally lost. If you're facing this and struggling with your worst fears, then do hold on. This is probably just a temporary setback. With kind and patient support, some rest, and a new look at things, you and your child can understand this as a small interruption along the journey of recovery. Help them realize that setbacks must not negate all their efforts, destroying their belief in themselves. Encourage them to view setbacks as part of a learning curve and try not to overreact.

Watching out for the vulnerable times

You'll be wise to look out for events that could threaten their recovery – vulnerable times often highly charged with emotion, such as friendship difficulties, the break-up of a boyfriend–girlfriend relationship, losing a job, exam pressures, or results disappointment. The serious illness or death of a close friend or relative is also a major challenge for someone who has struggled with their emotions. Sadly these events are part of life, but if your child is coming through self-harming or is newly recovered, then it's good to keep an eye out for these vulnerable times and to increase your level of care.

Parent to Parent

Recognizing the vulnerable times, times when she's more at risk of self-harm, and knowing not necessarily the trigger but the build-up is very important for us to identify, particularly in recovery when the scars are fading. Now she's tried to break the feeling that scars equal "I'm here and I'm hurting." She thinks the title you give yourself is important. She now calls herself a "recovering self-harmer" so that she's not a failure, either as a self-harmer or if she slips up, and this takes a lot of the pressure off her, she says, and a lot of guilt away so that she can move forward at her own pace. She says she gave herself permission not to try to address self-harm now as she's been sitting exams, and as a result she's managed not to harm, which makes her feel quite proud. She says she's lucky, as she's had a lot of encouragement.

Johanna

Living life free from self-harm is achievable

Please remember that living life free from self-harm is achievable. At ABC, we hear from people who have been recovered for decades, some of whom we've supported. For me and for my daughters, sustained recovery is based on their courage, their determination to be well and to live a good, full, and happy life again. It's also about the professional support they've received and, according to them, the love and support from their family and a few close friends. But most importantly, it's about them learning to know themselves and their vulnerable times, to take small risks in life, to learn how to cope differently and withstand difficulties as they mature. It's about them recognizing their personal achievements and surviving all the bad times, so I'm very proud of them. Here's what one of my daughters wrote:

Dealing with self-harm alone feels like a never-ending cycle of torment and shame. Part of you wants to confide in someone and share the burden, but the other half wants to hold on to the secret, afraid of what people might say or the shock it would create. Letting someone in is a big step; it's not an easy decision but can be the start of the journey to recovery. My mum has been an influential part of my recovery, and I don't think I would have experienced such progress if it weren't for her help. I began self-harming in hospital as a result of being confined to a bed for six weeks with no interaction with the real world except through letters and visitors. My mum was understandably sad and hurt for me, but she could empathize with my reasons. She knew how alone and isolated I was. It comforted me to know that she understood the emotions behind the physical act, even if she could not at first comprehend the significance of the harming itself. I think this is crucial – being interested in why your child is self-harming and the emotional triggers that have driven them to this point. I attempted to explain to my family the release self-harming gave me at a time when my emotions were too complex to process and it all felt overwhelming. Unfortunately, some people couldn't cope with the idea of my harming as a physical release and refused to accept it as a coping mechanism. I found this refusal to listen to me hard to bear; it ignited my feelings of shame and made me withdraw further.

I think listening without judgment is so important, as it helps the sufferer to voice their pain and end the cycle of private turmoil. It may be difficult to listen to your child describe how harming themselves helps and a part of you may even feel embarrassed, but it's important that you don't show these feelings. Self-harm is a cry for help, not an act of attention seeking or a phase, and I think part of being a parent is responding to your child's emotional needs without judgment or comment. My mum helped me to identify the triggers for a self-harm episode, factors such as: lack of sleep, lack of food, feeling overwhelmed, a difficult situation, stress, and anxiety, and helped me find ways to prevent an episode. I've learned that going to sleep is often a good way to diffuse my difficult feelings and in some way cheats the mind by shutting down and restarting.

I found I tended to get into a state and my feelings overtook my reasoning. My family helped me to find perspective and to look for a solution when it all seemed so overwhelming. I used to find it difficult to see a way out of my problems; my mum would reassure me and comfort me first by calmly and rationally helping me to identify a solution. My family always says there's a solution to everything, which really comforted me and made me realize that sharing my feelings was the first step to breaking the cycle of self-harm. This has helped me to identify ways in which I can calm myself down, often helping to prevent an episode. Having the strategies in place to diffuse my feelings is crucial to recovery and it sometimes helps to have them written down. For example: allowing yourself to cry and to release emotion, finding a focus (such as cleaning your room, finding someone and talking to them, going for a walk, or having a sleep) and then rewarding yourself, doing something nice for you. My family taught me how to safeguard myself for the future.

It is hard to find a way of coping that matches the release that self-harm gives, but exercise can provide a good alternative: running, cycling, or kick-boxing, even just using a punch bag. People forget that a lot of anger lies behind self-harming, and it's this anger that often creates the need to self-harm. Rather than suggesting alternatives without giving any thought to the complex emotions involved in self-harm, think about ways to counteract feelings of anger, guilt, frustration, loneliness, and anxiety, and talk it through with your child. It helped me to know that my mum was interested in me and was dedicated enough to want to help properly rather than being involved half-heartedly in my recovery.

It also helped that my family didn't pressurize me into stopping self-harming immediately; my mum realized that recovery was a process and would inevitably include some backward steps. I did experience a couple of relapses and afterwards felt very guilty and initially worried about the disappointment I'd cause. However, I found only reassurance and support, which spurred me on to recovery. Self-harm is an accumulation of many negative and dark feelings so it's crucial to counteract this with praise, encouragement, and love.

Imogen

Appendix: First Aid Chart

Type of injury	Home treatment	Emergency care
Surface cuts	• Clean the wound first with an antiseptic treatment. • Allow to dry and then cover with a plaster or dressing. • Check the wound from time to time and change the dressing if necessary.	• Seek medical help if there is an embedded object in the wound.
Deeper cuts	• Hold the flesh together. If necessary use self-closure strips. • Once closed cover with a sterile dressing. • Don't use antiseptic cream as this will prevent closure of the wound. • Regularly check the wound, re-dressing when needed. • Look out for any signs of infection such as red, inflamed skin or swelling. • Pain relief might need to be administered. • Watch for signs of shock. Symptoms can include: yawning and sighing; colour loss from the face; cold, clammy skin; a weak or rapid pulse; breathing that's shallow and fast; and fainting.	• Seek medical help if blood loss continues. • Keep applying pressure on the wound. • Use a clean cloth or clean fingers (disposable gloves). • If the injury is to a limb then raise it, support it, and bandage it.

Type of injury	Home treatment	Emergency care
Burns	• For minor burns, run the affected area under cool water to prevent tissue damage. Do this within the first 20 minutes. • Keep cooling the skin with lukewarm water for between 10 and 30 minutes. • Cover the burn with a sterile dressing or cling film or even a clean plastic bag. • Don't apply any creams or lotions. • Don't attempt to burst any blisters that might have developed.	• If the burn is deep or larger than a postage stamp, seek professional medical help.
Overdoses	• Get information about what substance has been taken and how long ago. • Look for packaging and containers, and collect anything that might have been used for the overdose, giving them to the paramedics. • Don't make them vomit.	• Ring the emergency services (or drive them to hospital if that's faster), letting the paramedics know as much detail as you can provide.

Type of injury	Home treatment	Emergency care
Unconsciousness	• Open their airway by placing one hand on the forehead and using two fingers to lift the chin. • Look to see if their chest rises and falls. • Listen for breathing. • Feel for their breath on your cheek. • Be ready to give rescue breaths and chest compressions if necessary. • If unconscious but breathing normally put them in the recovery position.	• Ring for an ambulance immediately or if alone get help after administering emergency rescue breaths and/or chest compressions.

This table of first aid is intended as a useful quick reference guide for home treatment and is not a substitute for professional medical care. It's recommended you take a first aid course and seek preparatory advice from the following UK organizations: NHS Direct (www.nhsdirect.nhs.uk); the Red Cross (www.redcross.org.uk); and St John's Ambulance (www.sja.org.uk).

Notes

1. The incidence of self-harm has continued to rise since the 1970s. See the NICE guidelines for self-harm, 2004: http://guidance.nice.org.uk/CG16/niceguidance/pdf/English

2. See Horrocks, J., "Self Poisoning and Self Injury in Adults", *Clinical Medicine*, 2(6), 2002, pages 509–512.

3. Fortune, S., Sinclair, J., and Hawton, K., "Adolescents' Views on Prevention of Self-harm, Barriers to Help-Seeking for Self-harm and How Quality of Life Might be Improved: A Qualitative & Quantitative Study", Oxford: Centre for Suicide Research, University of Oxford, 2005.

4. *Truth Hurts – Report of the National Inquiry into Self-Harm among Young People*, The Mental Health Foundation, 2006.

5. Fox, C. and Hawton, K., *Deliberate Self-Harm in Adolescence*, London, 2004, page 18.

6. *Truth Hurts*, page 39.

7. NICE guidelines, 2004.

8. The concept of adolescent egocentrism was first suggested by psychologist David Elkind. See Elkind, D., "Egocentrism in Adolescence", *Child Development*, 38(4), 1967, pages 1025–1034.

9. Hauser, S. T. and Bowlds, M. K., "Stress, Coping and Adaptation within Adolescence: Diversity and Resilience", in Feldman, S. and Elliott, G. (Eds), *At the Threshold*, Cambridge: Harvard University Press, 1990, pages 388–413.

10. Sachesse, U., Vonderheyde, S., and Huether, G., "Stress Regulation and Self-mutilation", *American Journal of Psychiatry*, 159(4), 2002, page 672.

11. New, A., Talbot, P., Siever, L., *et al.*, "Brain Serotonin Transporter Distribution in Subjects with Impulsive Aggressivity", *American Journal of Psychiatry*, 162(5), pages 915–923.

12. Fortune,S. A., and Hawton, K., "Suicide and deliberate self-harm in children and adolescents" (Symposium: Adolescent medicine), *Paediatrics and Child Health*, 17:11, Elsevier, 2007.

13. *Diagnostic and Statistical Manual of Mental Disorders (DSM-IV-TR)*, fourth edition, text revision, Washington D.C.: American Psychiatric Association, 2000, pages 589, 594–595.

14. *Truth Hurts*, page 41

15. Bryant-Waugh, R. and Lask, B., *Eating Disorders: A Parents' Guide*, London: Penguin, 1999. (A 2004 edition published by Routledge is also available.)

16. *Truth Hurts*, page 38.

17. Association of American Publishers, "Treating and Preventing Adolescent Mental Health Disorders, What We Know and What We Don't Know", 2005.

18. The NHS Information Centre: www.ic.nhs.uk

19. Lilley, R., Owens, D., Horrocks, J., *et al.*, "Hospital care and repetition following self-harm: multicentre comparison of self-poisoning and self-injury", *The British Journal of Psychiatry*, 192, 2008, pages 440–445.

20. Taylor T. L., Hawton K., Fortune S., *et al.*, "Attitudes towards clinical services among people who self-harm: systematic review", *The British Journal of Psychiatry*, 2009, page 106.

21. The NHS Information Centre: www.ic.nhs.uk/pubs/provisionalmonthlyhes

22. Nadkarni A., Parkin A., Dogra N., *et al.*, "Characteristics of children and adolescents presenting to accident and emergency

departments with deliberate self-harm", *Journal of Accident and Emergency Medicine*, 17(2), 2000, pages 98–102.

23. Wood A., Trainor G., Rothwell J., *et al.*, "Randomized trial of group therapy for repeated deliberate self-harm in adolescents", *Journal of the American Academy of Child and Adolescent Psychiatry*, 40(11), 2001, pages 1246–1253.

24. Ibid.

25. Linehan, M. M., *Skills Training Manual for Treating Borderline Personality Disorder*, New York and London: The Guilford Press, 1993.

26. Self-Help Network (2002), cited in Smith, A. and Clarke, J., "Self-Harm Self Help/Support Groups", The Mental Health Foundation, 2003, page 2.

27. Young, J. and Williams, C. L. (1987), cited in Smith, A. and Clarke, J., "Self-Harm Self Help/Support Groups", page 3.

28. Mental Health Foundation: http://www.mentalhealth.org.uk/help-information/mental-health-a-z/R/recovery

29. *Truth Hurts*, pages 61ff.

Suggested Reading

Bryant-Waugh, Rachel and Lask, Bryan, *Eating Disorders: A Parents' Guide*, London: Penguin, 1999 (a 2004 edition published by Routledge is also available).

Dawson, Dee, *Anorexia and Bulimia: A Parent's Guide to Recognising Eating Disorders and Taking Control*, London: Vermilion, 2001.

Hawton, Keith and Fox, Claudine, *Deliberate Self-Harm in Adolescence*, London: Jessica Kingley, 2004.

The Mental Health Foundation, *The Truth About Self-Harm*, London, 2006.

Motz, Anna (ed.), *Managing Self-Harm: Psychological Perspectives*, Hove: Routledge, 2009.

Princess Royal Trust for Carers, *Mental Health and the Triangle of Care*, 1991, http://www.carers.org/news/mental-health-and-triangle-care

Smith, Jane, *The Parent's Guide to Eating Disorders*, Oxford: Lion Hudson, 2011.

Spandler, Helen and Warner, Sam (eds), *Beyond Fear and Control: Working With Young People Who Self-Harm*, Herefordshire: PPS, 2007.

Sutton, Jan, *Healing the Hurt Within*, Oxford: How To Books, 2007.

National Institute for Health and Clinical Excellence (NICE)

NICE is a group working within the UK health system to produce guidelines for the treatment of all kinds of health issues. Working from research findings, it recommends best practice for treatment. Versions are published for medical professionals, patients, and their families.

NICE guidelines on self-harm – information for the public (including patients and their carers): http://guidance.nice.org.uk/CG16/PublicInfo/pdf/English

NICE guidelines on self-harm – quick reference guide: http://guidance.nice.org.uk/CG16/QuickRefGuide/pdf/English

NICE guidelines on eating disorders – information for the public (including patients and their carers): http://guidance.nice.org.uk/CG9/PublicInfo/pdf/English

NICE guidelines on eating disorders – quick reference guide: http://guidance.nice.org.uk/CG9/QuickRefGuide/pdf/English

Useful Contacts

UK-based organizations

Anorexia and Bulimia Care (ABC)
National organization that supports all who suffer because of eating disorders and related self-harm. Provides information, literature, advice, and support, as well as two unique befriending services (one for sufferers and one for parents of sufferers) that match someone struggling with an eating disorder to someone who has had experience of recovery, in order to support and encourage them.

Parent Support Line: 03000 11 12 13 (option 1)
Email: parentsupport@anorexiabulimiacare.org.uk
Sufferer Support Line: 03000 11 12 13 (option 2)
Email: sufferersupport@anorexiabulimiacare.org.uk
Self-harm Support Line: 03000 11 12 13 (option 3)
Email: selfharmsupport@anorexiabulimiacare.org.uk
Website: www.anorexiabulimiacare.org.uk

British Association for Counselling and Psychotherapy (BACP)
An organization that you can contact for details of practitioners in the UK.

Tel: 01455 88 33 00
Website: www.bacp.co.uk

Care for the Family
A national charity that aims to promote strong family life and to help those who face family difficulties.

Tel: 029 2081 0800
Email: mail@cff.org.uk
Website: www.careforthefamily.co.uk

The Institute of Psychiatry

The largest academic community in Europe devoted to the study and prevention of mental health problems. Its Eating Disorders Unit provides a range of high-quality services for patients of all ages, and across the spectrum of eating disorders.

Website: www.iop.kcl.ac.uk/sites/edu/?id=131

MIND

Provides information and advice and runs campaigns to promote and protect good mental health for everyone.

MINDinfoline: 0845 766 0163
Email: info@mind.org.uk
Website: www.mind.org.uk

National Self-Harm Network (NSHN)

Aims to empower individuals to explore reasons for their self-harm and to seek appropriate professional help. NSHN now equally supports friends, families, and carers of individuals who self-harm. It also aims to raise awareness of self-harm, its underlying causes, triggers, and the many ways to offer support. Provides training to professional organizations, schools, universities, charities, and user groups.

Tel: 0800 622 6000
(Thur–Sat 7 p.m.–11 p.m.; Sun 6.10 p.m.–10.30 p.m.)
Email: support@nshn.co.uk
Website: http://www.nshn.co.uk

NHS Direct

Tel: 0845 4647 (every day, twenty-four hours a day)
Website: http://www.nhsdirect.nhs.uk

Rethink

Leading mental health organization that works to help those affected by severe mental illnesses to recover a better quality of life.

Provides services and support, and campaigns for change through greater awareness and understanding.

Rethink's National Advice Service provides advice about schizophrenia, bipolar disorder, and other mental illness as well as related issues including legal rights and benefits.

Tel: 0845 456 0455 (weekdays 10 a.m.–2 p.m.)

Email: advice@rethink.org

Website: www.rethink.org

SANE

Offers emotional support, crisis care, and detailed information to people experiencing mental health problems, their family, carers, health and other professionals.

SANELine: 0845 767 8000 (every day 6 p.m.–11 p.m.)

Website: www.sane.org.uk

Selfharm.co.uk

Started out of the work of LCET, a Christian charity based in Luton, Bedfordshire, UK. Since its beginnings in 1993, the charity has developed a strong and professional reputation for delivering caring, child-centred work that focuses on the emotional and social needs of all young people. Selfharm.co.uk is a safe, pro-recovery site for communicating with others and expressing your experiences through the use of video blogs, stories, poetry, and art.

Email: info@selfharm.co.uk

Website: www.selfharm.co.uk

United Kingdom Council for Psychotherapy (UKCP)

Regional lists of psychotherapists are available free of charge.

Tel: 020 7014 9955

Website: www.psychotherapy.org.uk

YoungMinds

Provides information that helps children and young people cope with difficult feelings. Helps with a variety of concerns about children, including depression, behavioural problems, anxiety, and many others.

Parents' helpline: 0808 802 5544

Website: www.youngminds.org.uk

Organizations based outside the UK

American Self-Harm Information Clearinghouse (ASHIC)

Educates the general public and medical professionals about the phenomenon of self-harm. Disseminates clear, concise, and accurate information about self-harm to improve the treatment that sufferers receive from hospitals, physicians, therapists, and their own families and friends.

Tel: 206-604-8963 (in the US)

Email: ashic@selfinjury.org

Website: www.selfinjury.org

Inspire Foundation (ReachOut.com)

Inspire's flagship service ReachOut.com increases young people's knowledge of mental health and well-being, increases their help-seeking skills, and ensures that they feel less alone.

Tel: +61 2 8029 7777 (in Australia)

Email: info@inspire.org.au

Website: www.inspire.org.au

INSYNC (Interdisciplinary National Self-Injury in Youth Network Canada)

Provides general information on self-harm for young people and their family and friends.

Website: http://www.insync-group.ca

Kids Helpline

A free, 24-hour counselling service for children and young people. Counselling is offered by phone, email and over the web. Counsellors respond to more than 6,000 calls each week about issues ranging from relationship breakdowns and bullying, to sexual abuse, homelessness, self-harm, suicidal thoughts, and drug and alcohol use.

Tel: 07 3369 1588 (in Australia)
Email: admin@boystown.com.au
Website: www.kidshelp.com.au

S.A.F.E. Alternatives

A treatment programme that has helped thousands of people successfully end self-injurious behaviour. A treatment team of experts uses therapy, education, and support to empower clients to identify healthier ways to cope with emotional distress.

Tel: 800-DONTCUT, 800-366-8288, 888-396-7988 (in the US)
Email: info@selfinjury.com
Website: www.selfinjury.com

SPINZ (Suicide Prevention Information New Zealand)

A non-government, national information service providing information and resources to promote safe and effective suicide prevention activities.

Tel: 09 300 7035 (in New Zealand)
Email: info@spinz.org.nz
Website: www.spinz.org.nz

Supporting Families in Mental Illness (Auckland)

Provides free support, education, and information about mental illness.

Support and info line: 09 378 9134 (in New Zealand)
Email: admin@SFAuckland.org.nz
Website: www.sfauckland.org.nz

Teen Mental Health

Develops application-ready training programmes, publications, tools and resources that can be applied across disciplines to enhance the understanding of adolescent mental health and mental disorders.

Tel: (902) 470-6598 (in Canada)

Email: info[at]teenmentalhealth.org

Web-based organizations

RecoverYourLife.com

One of the biggest self-harm support communities on the internet. It also supports people with eating disorders and those dealing with abuse and other issues. The site contains articles, forums, chat, and live help, and is run by supporters to help people wanting to recover from self-harm.

Website: www.recoveryourlife.com

TheSite.org

Aims to be the first place that young adults turn to when they need support and guidance through life. Its fundamental belief is that all young people have the capacity to make their own decisions and life choices, provided they have access to high quality, impartial information and advice.

Tel: 020 7250 5700 (in the UK)

Website: www.thesite.org/healthandwellbeing/mentalhealth/selfharm